LABYRINTH WALKING

LABYRINTH WALKING

PATTERNS OF POWER

PATRICIA TELESCO

CITADEL PRESS
Kensington Publishing Corp.
www.kensingtonbooks.com

CITADEL PRESS books are published by

Kensington Publishing Corp.
850 Third Avenue
New York, NY 10022

All Kensington titles, imprints, and distributed lines are available at special quantity discounts for bulk purchases for sales promotions, premiums, fund raising, educational, or institutional use. Special book excerpts or customized printings can also be created to fit specific needs. For details, write or phone the office of the Kensington special sales manager: Kensington Publishing Corp., 850 Third Avenue, New York, NY 10022, attn: Special Sales Department, phone 1-800-221-2647.

Citadel Press and the Citadel logo are trademarks of Kensington Publishing Corp.

First printing June 2001

10   9   8   7   6   5   4   3   2   1

Printed in the United States of America

Library of Congress Control Number: 2001092640

ISBN 0-8065-2217-8

For: Rowan and Walker, Don and Dee, Dawn and Todd, Lena and Suzanne, Wade and Dianne—all of whom have guided me through my spiritual labyrinth, and often walked beside me with support, wisdom, gentle kindness, and love to make that path less long and difficult. Thank you seems a very small phrase for having learned how to "fix it" and how to trust, but I offer thanks with a full and grateful heart. Fair Winds and Sweet Waters!

CONTENTS

PART TWO: MAGICKAL MOTIFS

Illustrations

PREFACE

Labyrinth walking is an activity that anyone of any belief system can undertake. Religious systems as different as Christianity and Buddhism have used the sacred patterns presented in this book as spiritual tools. These tools help the soulful seeker achieve various goals: establishing prayerful attitudes, deepening meditative states, creating a strong spiritual focus, and ultimately discovering how to fulfill our divine purpose while establishing personal wholeness.

So, while I've written this book for magickally minded folk, there is no reason that people of a different persuasion can't adapt the activities herein to better suit their beliefs. In fact, I encourage everyone to do just that. The more you personalize any activity, the more meaningful it will be, and the more powerfully it will manifest in your life.

I would also like to reiterate here that my version of magick and Wicca is very eclectic. It is but one way to walk this particular spiritual path. It is my pattern of power. So, nothing here is carved in stone or hedges (other than the labyrinth). Let your heart guide you.

For more information about this and other metaphysical subjects, refer to www.loresinger.com, clubs.yahoo.com/clubs/folkmagicwithtrishtelesco, or, www.witchvdx.com

Labyrinth in Rheims Cathedral, circa 1240 A.D.

INTRODUCTION

The Labyrinth is a model of spiritual cosmology . . .
                                        —Keith Critchlow

Throughout history humans have used symbols, signs, and patterns to give physical form to concepts that seem to transcend language. If an idea was too moving, too mysterious, or too vast for verbalization, people turned to pictographs to represent what mere words could not convey. Even then, the pictograph was but a shadow of something far greater, of something that attempted to speak to our higher self and soul.

Among these sacred patterns we find three appearing and reappearing in a wide variety of cultural settings. It is toward these three—labyrinths, mazes, and mandalas—that *Labyrinth Walking* directs its focus. It does so in the effort to answer one specific question: What do these inspired designs, and others like them, have to do with our spiritual pursuits? After all, many people have tried solving mazes in the Sunday paper or physically walked a hedge style labyrinth and never considered it remotely "magickal."

Labyrinth Walking responds to this inquiry and many more by sharing the history, facts, folklore, and superstitions surrounding the mysterious motifs portrayed in the world's labyrinths, mazes, and mandalas. In studying this material it became quickly evident that spiritual and magickal potential saturates these designs. From the Chartres labyrinth in France that was used for penance to the Native American labyrinths in the southwestern United States, these paths to a center point are a maker's mark of sorts— the ancients believed they embody the patterns of all creation, all knowledge, and all mysteries, in physical form. They are, in effect, the path back to the center of our being and our Source.

Similar to the labryinth, mandalas encircle center point proportionately, using symbols to convey concepts not easily described with mere words: unity, perfection, place versus time, movement versus stillness, the within and without. By so doing, the mandala emphasizes the relationship between god/dess and the world, the physical versus the material, the whole in the part. The point of the mandala symbolizes the Source and an anchor for our soul so we don't get lost in the labyrinth of life. This point is the nucleus of our being and our genesis to which we strive to return.

Mazes symbolize the decision-making process of our lives. The intricate windings and illusions are specifically designed to stress the right-brain/left-brain interaction that either separates us from, or draws us to, this very same Source or point. So, in studying mazes, mandalas, and other sacred configurations, and slowly unraveling their secrets, we cannot help but learn new and interesting things about ourselves and the Universe in all its wonder.

More importantly, we also can learn to apply these sacred designs as tools for re-patterning our lives in more positive, empowering, and spiritual ways. Each labyrinth, maze, or mandala is one path—a road by which humankind can begin reconnecting with Spirit, releasing magickal power, and awakening our psychic selves. By purposefully and mindfully walking down this roadway, and giving ourselves over to its pattern, we liberate a specific type of mystical energy into our aura and into our lives—the energy of wholeness. The lion's share of *Labyrinth Walking* is written to help you do just that.

Through the pages of this book you'll discover ways of making your own power patterns. Whether you need to enhance your love life, decrease stress, change a negative cycle, improve finances, augment creativity, quiet your mind, or shift your focus toward magickal matters, labyrinths, mazes, and mandalas offer many selections suited to your needs and goals. The trick is sifting through the vast assortment of imagery available and deciding on one or two that best represent your aspiration in manifested form.

Labyrinth Walking begins your journey at this decision-making point. Part One of this book gives you information on the importance of patterns in our lives. It explains what mazes, mandalas, and labyrinths are designed to do, and provides examples of common human situations in which to apply those potent patterns. From those illustrations it is but a short step to picking a design, finding a suitable medium through which to express your chosen energy pattern, and finally manifesting powerful, transformational magick!

Thankfully, there are many ways to release and activate the energy placed within these designs. You can draw the emblem as part of a charm or amulet. You can imagine the symbol in pathworking and visualization exercises. You can move through the pattern as part of a ritual, solve a maze to solve problems, grow the motif in a meditation garden, or design a labyrinth in stonework around your house for protection and ongoing positive energy. Better still, the design you choose need not come from a traditional labyrinth, mandala, or maze! With a little creativity the options become nearly endless, which bring us to Part Two of *Labyrinth Walking*.

Part Two is basically a dictionary of symbols. Here you'll find archetypal imagery that you can use in creating your own mazes, mandalas, and labyrinths, or adapting ones that need a little tweaking to meet your needs. From circles, squares, and triangles to runes and ancient magickal sigils, the patterns of power have been with us for a very long time. These simple

emblems touch the depths of our subconscious and superconscious mind to ignite the sparks of magick that abide there. Once
chosen, making and using the power pattern becomes the
process by which you release all that potential into every corner
of your reality.

Walk with me now through the pages of this book and into
the wonderful world of sacred patterns. Reclaim the designs that
house the answers you seek. Then transform the cycles of your
life so they include a spiritual vision and patterned progression
toward a sense of peace, and an awareness of the Sacred in all
things. It's truly a-*mazing*!

PART ONE

CONJURED CONFIGURATIONS

As when in lofty Crete (so fame reports)
the Labyrinth of old, in winding walls
a mazy way inclos'd, a thousand paths
ambiguous and perplexed, by which the steps
should by an error indicate, untrac'd
be still deluded

—Aeneid V, 585–591

Labyrinth in the Abbey of St. Bertin, St. Omer

1

PATTERNS OF POWER

*And [paths] so cunningly contriv'd, with turnings round
about, that none but with a clew of thread could enter
in or out.*

—John Aubrey, *Remaines* (1686)

What is it about a pattern that creates or motivates specific energies? How do patterns effect our conscious, subconscious, and superconscious mind? These two questions are the cornerstone to understanding the power of labyrinths, mazes, and mandalas. The answer to this query, however, is nowhere near as illusive as is solving a difficult maze. It's right under our noses, being expressed in our daily reality all the time!

Think about your life for a moment. Isn't it filled with patterns? Isn't it filled with habits that you think very little about? If you sleep on the same side of the bed each night, follow a specific morning routine, or drive to the supermarket by the same road each time, you're creating a pattern. That pattern expresses part of who you are and the way you think.

But what happens when the pattern is disrupted? Say, for example, your usual route to work is cut off and you have to take a detour. Do you find your whole day seems "off" some-how? That's because the rhythm provided by your daily pattern creates a comfortable familiarity and certain black-and-white outlines in your life. When the pattern breaks temporarily, you have to adjust your energy. This adjustment takes time and, as if guided by Murphy's Laws, the amount of time is typically about as long as the disruption lasts!

When patterns break permanently, such as occurs in divorce or death, the adjustment period is much longer. Why? Because patterns like those were very meaningful. Other configurations, like a bad habit, may have been with us for years, so it only makes sense that calibrating to a new one would be onerous. Life, however, is filled with change no matter how much we'd like to stay with a status quo. So we need to find coping mech-anisms to handle the new and emerging patterns in our reality effectively.

Then too, what about the negative cycles in our lives? Some people, for example, are repeatedly drawn into unproductive or unhealthy relationships. One leads to another, and to another. The harmful cycle actually seems to propagate itself. Why? It's the law of like attracting like on a very intimate level. Anger brings anger, prejudice creates prejudice, insecurity breeds inse-curity. It has happened, and will continue to happen, far more often than any of us would like until we purposefully and mind-fully break the pattern's power over us.

One of our ancestors' creative answers to problems and situ-ations like these was making (and using) labyrinths, mazes, mandalas, and other sacred designs. No matter the culture or time frame, evidence suggests that the ancients were very pur-poseful in developing each scheme. They trusted that power resided in the image, or felt that energy was invoked by the symbol and its significance.

For example, Aborigines traced certain patterns as one way of honoring and communing with the Ancestors. The act was said to improve the worshiper's meditative state, and actually open the veil between the worlds so the Ancestors could communicate clearly. Similarly, there are some esoteric traditions in which labyrinth walking was part of initiation proceedings. This activity added physical movement to what the Aborigines were doing so that the whole person became part of the sacred pattern, and his or her spirit would be awakened for the ensuing ritual.

In both aforementioned illustrations the way of creating a pattern and the way of reaching the goal was just as important as the goal itself. The creation process might have been timed by a lunar cycle, or the way of reaching the goal limited to one specific path. In either case, these ways, these paths, represented every twist, turn, obstacle, and opportunity life had to offer. They also represented the roadway back to the god/dess. There is absolutely nothing that keeps us from following this example and applying it to our magickal pursuits today.

By creating labyrinths, mandalas, and mazes, the ancients were trying to illustrate a truism that modern-minded folk are also starting to re-acknowledge. All of life can become a sacred pattern that guides us toward a reunion with Spirit. When we don't recognize or activate this aspect of life's potential our souls remain lost in old patterns, old ways of thinking, old ways of being, and often lose sight of the Sacred powers altogether.

Each person is in the process of making the choice between spiritual apathy and aliveness every day, frequently without knowing it. I present this choice to you now within the framework of this book. Whether you want to deal more effectively with the constantly changing world, create new patterns that will help you become a truly magickal person in thought and deed, or strengthen the positive patterns you've already created, walking a sacred path, following the sacred pattern, is one answer to that desire.

Please note in reading the rest of this book that I will be using the phrase "labyrinth walking" as a broad catch-all phrase to alleviate repetition. It is meant to include all the potential applications for sacred patterns in our lives.

Personal and Planetary Auras

Before we can start creating sacred patterns for ourselves, others, or the earth we first have to understand the ones that already exist. Each person has an energy pattern in his or her aura. The earth also has a special pattern as evidenced by ley lines, vortexes, and power centers. These pre-existing patterns need to be treated respectfully in order for labyrinth walking to truly have a positive effect.

To understand the "whys" of this, think of what would happen if a city randomly laid out new roads without looking to see what was already in place. It would create a terrible mess. Similarly, the patterns we've created in our lifetime, and those housed by the earth, can't just be torn up and tossed aside thoughtlessly. While the changes from such an action would certainly be dramatic, the results wouldn't necessarily be positive because of what I call energy shock.

Energy shock in one's aura or on a planetary scale is very similar to what happens to the human body when it goes into shock. Dramatic changes in the pattern may create substantial trauma in life's network, possibly to the point where everything starts shutting down. A good example of discernible energy shock is a war-torn area where ley lines have been bloodied. The residual feelings that psychics receive in such regions isn't pleasant, and often comes across as a spiritually "dead" zone. Thus we need to create and walk our labyrinths gently and mindfully.

The next logical question becomes, how do we familiarize ourselves with the energy patterns of a person, place, or thing? That's not necessarily an easy question to answer because each person responds to symbolism differently. Initially, I suggest you begin to think of yourself and all things as part of the planetary (and universal) "body" so that you become more aware of the sacredness and interconnectedness of all things. Not one person on this planet can breathe without effecting someone or something else around him or her. That's how tightly life's patterns overlap.

Secondly, open your eyes—both the physical and spiritual ones. Take long walks and really look at the world around you. Patterns are everywhere: in your home, in art, in flower petals, in the stars. The more you make yourself aware of these tangible patterns, the easier it will become to recognize similar ones on an auric level.

Third, get into the habit of meditating regularly, even if for only five to ten minutes a day. Meditation is one key to successful labyrinth walking because it opens your spirit and mind to new possibilities and new perspectives. It also quiets the soul long enough for the Sacred to get a word in edgewise. In either case, I can nearly guarantee that even after only one week of habitual meditation, you'll notice your overall awareness improving and stress decreasing.

By the way, you can meditate with plants, animals, stones, or other people to help yourself become more attuned to the patterns each bears. Here's an exercise you can try yourself with different items:

1. Pick out the object whose energy patterns you want to better understand.
2. Ensure yourself some quiet time (ten minutes) and get comfortable, keeping that object within arm's reach.
3. Take three very deep breaths, inhaling and exhaling slowly. Try to keep these breaths even.
4. Pay particular attention to your stress levels and focus in Step 3. If you still feel distracted or tense, continue breathing in an all-connected manner until the discomfort disappears.
5. Take the chosen item in hand and close your eyes. Consider its shape, size, aroma (if applicable), and how it feels in your hand (cool, warm, sharp, smooth, etc.).
6. Now, keep your focus on the item and breathe again as before but direct the energy of your breath into that item.

Does it feel differently now? Is it warmer? Itchy? Tingly? Sensations like this indicate that you're doing this exercise correctly.

7. Be patient. Our psychic self isn't used to getting a real workout. It may take a couple of tries before you sense anything from the item.

8. When you do start sensing an item's aura, it won't always come through a feeling. You may hear something, see something in your mind's eye, smell something in the air, or whatever. Your psychic self will generally communicate through the sense (hearing, taste, touch, smell, sight) to which you respond most strongly. So, if you were holding a stone and its energy pattern was one most suited to increasing power/energy (quartz is a good example) you might feel static, or get the mental image of a battery, for example. But don't worry, your mind knows you very well—it will always provide symbolism to which you can easily relate.

9. Make notes of your experience. This way you can follow any successful "pattern" created by the activity in the future! Also make note of the message you received from that item. This information will generally indicate the way in which it will function best in both your labyrinth walking activities, and in your magick.

Fourth, start trusting your instincts (that little voice deep within). Labyrinth walking has a lot to do with self-awareness and conviction. If we don't believe in ourselves, in our magick, the journey becomes difficult—we'll stumble or stop, feeling lost and confused. And, if we don't have faith in the pattern of power that resides in our own soul, trying to discover it in anything else is pretty much an exercise in futility! To learn the pattern, to trust the pattern, you must first know yourself.

Finally, for those people who need or want some kind of visual confirmation of a pre-existing pattern, I suggest trying pendulum or dowsing work. Both a pendulum and a dowsing rod will respond to the patterns of power. Pendulums will swing in a particular manner to reveal information (like spinning clockwise over an open chakra). Here's how to make and use one at home:

1. Take a circular ring like a wedding band (it's best if this has no stone in it) and attach it to a length of string that roughly equals your middle finger-to-elbow measurement.
2. If the ring has a stone in it, make sure the stone is directly down from the area where you've secured the string. This ensures that the weight of the stone won't influence your results.
3. Go to an area that you think a ley line or power center exists. Stop and lie down on the earth, placing the elbow of your strong hand on the ground.
4. Hold the pendulum in your strong hand, steadying it over the ground.
5. Close your eyes and focus on the energy around you. Try to keep your arm very still so you don't influence the pendulum by your movements.
6. After a few minutes, open your eyes and see what the pendulum is doing, if anything. Back and forth movements can indicate a ley line, while circles tend to indicate a power center or vortex.

Dowsing rods dip at power points and often vibrate near a ley line. You can make your own dowsing rod out of any Y-shaped branch you find (hold the forked end in your hands). Pendulums in metal and crystal can be purchased at many New Age outlets. An online resource for both items can be found at http://globus.elonet.com.il/~eden

Making Your Own Patterns

Once we've awakened and attuned ourselves to life's patterns, we can then start thinking about labyrinth walking in more concrete terms. There's just one problem. Not all of us can travel the world to use an existing maze, mandala, or labyrinth! For those who have the ability to do so, a list of some more famous sites is provided in Appendix B.

For those who cannot, this section will give you ideas on how to create your own sacred patterns no matter where you live. More examples will be included in the next three chapters.

Grow It!

Anyone with a windowsill or garden area can grow a sacred pattern. To do this, you need to carefully lay out the space you have available, putting various-colored plants in specific spots to create the pattern desired. For example, a simple four-color motif of yellow or white, red or orange, purple or blue, and green or brown can become the points of an elemental garden. Put yellow flowers at the east, red in the south, purple in the west, and green in the north. The result is a miniature sacred space that's vibrant with life!

Another fun option with indoor and outdoor motif gardening is a fairy garden. These are designed specifically to attract positive, playful devic entities into your life. Fairy gardens are typically laid out in the form of a circle (note that naturally grown circles of mushrooms or trees are often called fairy rings). Some of the flowers and herbs you can consider that grow in this simple mandala are rosemary, thyme, baby's breath, mosses, clover, lily of the valley, hawthorn, and primrose. For the center point of the circle, get a small doll house or something similar in which the wee folk can live once they come-a-calling!

While you cannot "walk" indoor and smaller gardens, you

can meditate near them, let the pattern of energy grow into maturity for manifestation, and even cook with edible self-grown items to internalize the pattern of power from both the plant and the garden's design.

Stone Work

The abundance of crystals available these days makes it easy to create a stone montage for your labyrinth-walking efforts. Place small stones around your home like bric-a-brac, but patterned in such a way as to draw in positive energy. For example, I keep tiny stones on my altar in formation of a clockwise-turning spiral. If the stones are small enough, glue them on a piece of paper and carry the energy with you!

On a larger scale, the standing stone megaliths around the world are an excellent example of sacred patterning. You can make these in miniature on any table surface, or as the center point in your garden. If you have more land available, set up a full-sized version! Note that the ancient stone patterns sometimes formed a circle, straight lines, squares, and some were spoked like wheels. So, there's nothing that says you have to make a circle with your stones if another pattern is better suited to the energy you're trying to create, or the pattern that already exists in the land.

To cite a personal example, in doing some gardening recently I found two lovely 12-inch stones with interesting shapes, and several smaller pieces. I placed the large stones at the two corner points of two rose gardens, opposite one another in the back of the yard. The smaller pieces were spaced somewhat equally from one another moving up from the corner points toward the house (this created a squared-off U visually). Once in place, this simple arrangement immediately created a veil of power along the property line that I can sense. There it stands, extending its arms to the house like a guardian for my home and family.

Cloth

Draw or paint your sacred patterns on a piece of cloth of a suitable size and fabric so that it will handle your intended application. For example, if you're making a large walking pattern, I'd suggest fabric paint on canvas with some kind of water-proofing for longevity. White flat sheets are also ideal for large labyrinths. (If you use the right kinds of paints these are wash-able!) In either case, I suggest undertaking this activity bare-footed for two reasons. First, it puts your skin in direct contact with the energy design. Second, it will decrease wear and tear on the fabric.

Helpful Hint

Choose the colors of your labyrinth's plants, stones, fabric, paint, or paper according to your magickal goals. Remember that color has a wavelength—a pattern that provides sympa-thetic support for your efforts. Red is a good energy booster and also represents love, passion, and vitality. Orange is a friendly color that helps you reap what you've carefully sown. Yellow communicates, inspires, and motivates. Green is growth oriented, blue is peaceful, and purple accents magick focused on spirituality or leadership.

Smaller scraps of fabric are suited to making meditative wall hangings, charms, and amulets. These can be painted or embroi-dered with the pattern desired then hung, placed with clothing, or carried for ongoing power. If you like to sew, quilt a pattern, make a patterned ritual robe, altar cloth, or similar items so you surround yourself with the symbols of power!

Paper

Cardboard, construction paper, and writing paper all make good media for temporary labyrinths. Bear in mind though, that the finished product won't last as long as cloth, stone, or grown designs. Personally, I prefer vellum, which has an antique feel for making pocket-sized patterns that allow me to take the designated magick with me.

Large pieces of cardboard can be used at gatherings for one or two labyrinth walks (you will probably have to connect the pieces or lay them out like a puzzle, securing them in place with double-sided tape), and construction paper might make a nice backdrop for thematic meditative foci in a group setting. For example, perhaps the entire group could start at the center point of an outward-moving spiral on construction paper (for growing power) that ends in a complete circle (for unity). This design is very simple to draw, and it augments nearly any type of magick your group is creating!

Carving or Sculpting

For those with talents along these lines, there's absolutely no reason not to carve your labyrinths into wood, rock, or soapstone, or sculpt them in clay. We see examples of this throughout Europe in art and architecture, the second often having a protective quality ascribed to it.

What's wonderful about these media is that each allows you to express the pattern artistically and in three dimensions, which in turn also improves the results of the work. Think of it this way: a two-dimensional image is flat for all intensive purposes, where three dimensions come to life. That's also what you want for energy—for it to be lively! The more dimension you give to your magick the better.

Helpful Hint

Keep your purpose in mind all the while you make your labyrinth designs. This builds energy. See, the creative process makes something from nothing—in this case the pattern. As this pattern manifests in the medium you've chosen, it plants the right energy seeds for the pattern to manifest in your life. All that remains is for you to water the seeds—through meditation, spellcraft, walking, or whatever!

Sand or Dirt

While these two media might not come immediately to mind for labyrinth walking, they have lots of potential. Large tracts of land or dirt can be etched by foot or hand with sacred patterns, then walked (a good example of this is the crop circles). As you walk, remember you are making yourself part of the earth and part of that pattern. Focus on your goal and merging yourself into the whole.

When you're done, you can scoop up a handful of the dirt/sand and put it in a pouch. It is already charged with the energy of your purpose, so you can now carry it with you to help keep the energy moving and manifest the magick. Afterward, wipe the land clean so you can use it for another pattern later. Or, leave the pattern in place to bless the land, and let nature's hand scatter the energy.

For smaller-scale efforts, trace the desired design in a box of fine dirt or play sand as part of meditation and spellcraft! Trace circles within circles when trying to focus, or a square as part of a foundation spell (squares represent the earth element and foundations). Old wine boxes with tight-fitting boards work well for this option (you can often get them free from a nearby liquor store) as does a cake pan, food storage container (with lid to keep everything neatly inside), empty drawer, and so forth. If you wish, combine the personal sand box idea with crystals, akin to a zen rock garden that you can take with you everywhere and constantly repattern to mirror your goals!

Edible Patterns

Being a terminal kitchen witch, if I can find a way to mix magick with food, I do. Labyrinth walking has been no exception. Try patterning sliced hot dogs, sticky rice, mashed potatoes, and even a vegetable platter in metaphysically pleasing ways. Just make sure that the symbolic value of the edible and the pattern you're creating match one another. For example, baby carrots might be laid out like an eye to encourage "vision" or rice might be laid out on a bed of lettuce so it looks like a dollar sign to bring prosperity. When you eat, you internalize the power of the pattern!

Again, more examples of labyrinth making will be found in each section that follows in this book, with step-by-step designs that will help you fashion the right pattern to meet your needs and goals.

Walking the Path

Magickal patterning won't help much of anything if you don't do something with it! The symbolic importance of action, of taking that first step no matter its form, shouldn't be underestimated. This is an initiation of sorts. It marks the beginning of your desire for change, the beginning of your magick in manifested form, and the willingness to accept the energy you've designed. Nonetheless, all this doesn't happen without some forethought and preparation.

Most people don't go job hunting or to college without a plan. Heck, we barely take a day off without some type of plan! Labyrinth walking should also be a well-considered endeavor in your life. The following eleven steps will not only prepare you for your adventure in labyrinth walking, but will also help make it the most positive experience possible:

Eleven Steps for Walking the Sacred Pattern

1. *Preparation:* As with any type of magick, your state of mind is important to successful labyrinth walking. You shouldn't be tired, ill, out-of-sorts, angry, or otherwise out of balance in any way. So do a self-check before making or walking your labyrinth. If you're not at your best, it's often better to wait.

Some people like to fast for a short time before labyrinth walking (like one meal, if physically feasible). This acts as an offering of sorts, and it also begins the process of turning one's mind away from temporal matters. During this time they often pray, read a magickal book, or take part in some other type of spiritual activity to stress this goal.

Other people like to anoint themselves with a significant aromatic, take a cleansing bath or shower, chant, or meditate *before* beginning the pattern. Aromatics move into your aura to shift your awareness, and then carry that transformation on the walk via subtle aromatherapy. A cleansing bath or shower relaxes and purifies the body and spirit for communing with sacred powers. Chanting and meditation ready the mind and soul.

I personally use frankincense and myrrh oil on my chakras and then meditate for about ten minutes until I feel centered and focused, but you might not find this approach similarly helpful. Every person is different. You're going to have to go through a little old-fashioned "trial and error" to figure out which method(s) work best to get you in the right "space" for labyrinth walking.

2. *Relax:* Shake the tension out of your shoulders and arms. Tension is like a dam to magickal energy flows. Stress often indicates that your mind is focused on other things besides spiritual matters. The physical effect constricts and constrains your ability to really enjoy and integrate the labyrinth-walking experience. Some people find stretching before the activity helps, as does a gentle massage, a warm shower, or something else that you find similarly relaxing.

3. *Quiet Your Mind:* For most folks this translates into taking a few moments in meditation to prepare yourself for whatever lies ahead in the pattern. Try to "turn off" the mundane thoughts for a while and focus your soul on the Sacred and your magick. Let these two things working in tandem bring about the transformation desired by the patterning.

4. *Breathe Deeply:* In Indian thought prana (life's current) is directly related to rhythmic breathing. It also evokes creativity and insight by awakening the body centers (chakras) and by so doing liberates the superconscious self. Similarly in Egypt, Tibet, and China, breath represents the soul in motion. This is exactly what you want: an active, aware, alert spirit.

In keeping with this goal, keep your breaths slow, full, and even throughout your labyrinth walking activities. Connect each breath's cycle to the next like a giant circular mandala that bears positive energy to every cell in your body. If it helps, visualize your breath as sparkling white light so you can actually imagine the circle of energy you're creating with breath.

5. *Don't Anticipate:* While I'm certain you've chosen your labyrinth-walking activity for a specific purpose, try to release your expectations from the outset of the exercise. Instead, let the pattern's energy and purpose reveal itself as you go along. Why? Because sometimes what we think we need, and what we *really* need, are two different things. As one walks a sacred path, and follows a sacred pattern, those needs can make themselves known. If

you've closed yourself off by anticipating only a specific result from your walk, you might miss important messages from your subconscious, from the earth, from spirits, or from the Sacred Powers.

6. *Go Slowly:* Labyrinth walking is not a hurry-up proposition. Magick works outside of space and time, and rarely conforms itself to mundane schedules, so leave yourself plenty of time for whatever activity you have in mind. Gently remind yourself as you work that there's no need to rush here, and no need to try and keep up with anyone else's pace. Just like your spiritual path, the movement through any labyrinth-walking activity should be a stride with which you're comfortable—that feels wholly right. If at any point you start feeling uneasy stop and consider why, then adjust your body, mind, and spirit accordingly.

7. *Stay Focused:* Make a conscious effort to maintain your meditative state of mind. This will allow you to be more open and aware of the entire experience and what it means to you or your group. If you find that you get distracted by something temporal (like the phone ringing), it might be best to start the exercise over again.

Generally speaking a sacred pattern does not evoke its energies very well if you can't go from the beginning to the end uninterrupted, because the pattern builds the energy (akin to walking a set of stairs) from the foundation up. If time doesn't allow you to start over, at least take a few cleansing breaths and re-establish a heightened spiritual mind-frame. Briefly review what you thought, experienced, or sensed up to that point in the activity. This way when you move on, the rest is still fresh in your mind to make a more cohesive experience.

8. *Be Receptive:* A goodly portion of labyrinth walking is focused on remaining receptive to inspiration in all its forms. If you suddenly feel like dancing the pattern, singing as you go, stopping and praying for a while, or even following a totally different pattern than what you'd originally planned, do so!

Remember that the pattern is but a rough spiritual blueprint. You are the architect for magickal energy. Your thoughts and actions, your spiritual artistry, create the finishing touches on that design. This means that the final form and magick resulting from same is wholly up to you! Trust yourself and really listen to that little voice within.

9. *Stay Aware of Your Body:* It's very easy to lose sight of the physical in labyrinth walking, but if we remember that the keynote of the experience is restoring the balance, it's easier to stay in touch with our bodies. Even above the desire to maintain body-mind-spirit symmetry, our bodies can communicate a lot to us during labyrinth walking if we listen. Some people, for example, experience shivers, a sense of static, sudden bursts of laughing or crying, and other phenomena along the way. This happens because the pattern evokes various soul memories stored deep within. As those are awakened, activated, integrated, remembered, or released, there is a physical reaction.

Pay attention to these kinds of feelings so you can examine the whys of it afterward. It's an important part of the whole experience and will often reveal memories or feelings you've supressed, past lives, creative impulses, and other similar information that will prove very helpful to your growth as a magickal being.

10. *Make Notes of Your Experience:* If you don't already maintain a magickal journal, now's the time to start! You can tape your experiences and insights, log them in your computer, or write them in a handy diary. The form doesn't matter; the recording of this information does! By re-reading these logs you'll discover new perspectives, integrate many of the things you've learned, and also be able to observe your personal spiritual progress with more impartiality (humans tend to be their own worst critics in this regard).

Better still, this journal will chronicle your failures and successes with magickal patterning efforts. This way you can "tweak" those that didn't go as you might have wished. You can

also repeat those that really helped, or share them with someone else in need.

11. *Repeat the Walk or Try a New One:* Each journey in labyrinth
walking will be different. (You just have to trust me on this until
you begin trying the patterns yourself.) As mentioned in Step 4,
one simple pattern like that of a concentric square can elicit
completely different experiences from one attempt to the next,
simply based on your frame of mind, your needs, the atmosphere around you, the method of making the labyrinth (e.g.,
the media), and other similar internal and external factors.

For example, say that someone makes a symbol like a
squared-off spiral on paper and carries it to keep his or her feet
on the ground during those times when wishful thinking is
tempting. Specifically, this emblem is used when entering into a
new relationship so s/he doesn't let heart and desires overcome
reason and caution. And, for the sake of argument, say the pattern seemed to help with that situation.

Now, on another occasion the same person makes this pattern
again. S/he then suddenly finds him- or herself being more
aware of the body's gravity center and feeling more focused
rather than less romantic. Yes, these two things connect to being
grounded and rational, but are definitely a slightly different
manifestation, and one that was likely needed at that moment.

Repeating the pattern here (or on any occasion) could have
had two distinct outcomes. It will either serve to deepen that
pattern's meaning, energy, and manifesting power in your life,
or it will create a variant, expanded energy with which to work!
To my thinking, both sound pretty good.

Moving Out or Moving In; Moving Back
or Moving Forward?

Many patterns discussed in this book can be started in the
center or on the outer edge, walked clockwise or counterclock-

wise, backward or forward. For example, in a cloth maze you could easily walk to the middle and try to work your way outward, or begin at an outside opening and work inward. So, the question becomes, do you want to move in or out, to the right or to the left?

To answer this you're going to need to think about several things:

1. Are you trying to draw energy inward or move it out from yourself? Moving it out from the self (you are a nucleus) is symbolically supported by beginning in the middle of a design. Conversely, drawing energy inward to a point of manifestation and understanding (the center) usually starts externally on the edge of the pattern.
2. Are you trying to produce a positive or banish a negative? In many esoteric traditions, moving clockwise is considered conducive to creating "good vibrations" while moving counterclockwise diminishes unwanted influences and turns negativity around.
3. Is your magick focused on the past or future (such as healing memories or finding a life mate)? The past is best symbolized by the center of a pattern or by backward movement, and/or counterclockwise movement (turning back the hands of time). The future is best represented by the outer edge of a pattern, its completion point, forward and/or clockwise movement (moving the hands of time forward following the sun's natural movement through the sky).

In many instances you can combine these concepts to improve the symbolic value and effect. For example, start an energy-building pattern in the center and move clockwise as you go. Or banish a negative habit by moving counterclockwise from the center out, then reverse the pattern to attract positive energy in its place.

Adding Timing and Sensual Cues to the Walk

Humans use their senses as a way of interpreting and comprehending both the natural and supernatural worlds. In a magickal setting we rely on heightened senses to communicate goals and energies to our superconscious and to the Powers. Basically, one sense on top of another builds a multi-dimensional image. This becomes a sympathetic sensory design that neatly mirrors the magick you're creating. Therefore, each sense you can bring into the labyrinth-walking activity will geometrically improve the results.

One method that a lot of people find helpful is that of wearing costumes and masks. This helps you step out of yourself figuratively and into a new role better suited to the magick you're creating. The symbolic visual and physical effects of this process shouldn't be overlooked either.

Here are some other specific examples for you to try in your labyrinth-walking activities. Bear in mind that the goal represented by your pattern, your movements throughout (or creation of) that pattern, and your sensory cues should all be in harmony with one another and wholly meaningful to you. Otherwise you end up with a lot of mixed signals that act like astral static and interfere with the magickal flow.

AROMAS

Aromatherapy has recently come back into the public eye as an effective, non-intrusive way of improving a person's or place's vibrations. Sprinkle scented powder on the floor and use it as a walking pattern; open a window for fresh air (which symbolizes fresh perspectives); make an aromatic bug repellent for your grown labyrinths, and so forth.

Here's a list of aromatic correspondences to get you started. More information along these lines can be found in my book *The Herbal Arts*.

Aromatherapy Correspondences

Apple: health or joy
Berry (any): happiness and abundance
Cedar: fortitude and courage
Cinnamon: energy, the fire element
Coconut: purity, the water element
Ginger: success and victory
Jasmine: focus for meditation
Lavender: lifting depression; peace; the air element
Lemon: purification, friendship
Lilac: symmetry and oneness
Lotus: the goddess aspect
Mint: fresh outlooks; prosperity
Myrrh: banishing and cleansing
Orange: healing (especially relationships); money
Patchouli: the god aspect; the earth element
Rose: all types of love
Rosemary: improving the conscious mind
Sandalwood: spirituality and psychism
Vanilla: passion and devotion
Violet: protection (especially from ghosts)

To put this into an illustration, say you were designing an earth square to walk for grounding or to bring yourself in closer contact with the earth. You could anoint the cloth for this walk with patchouli oil to honor the earth element.

SIGHTS

What you see as you walk the labyrinth is also important. Just think of the old aphorism "seeing is believing" for a minute. What we see affects us deeply. So above and beyond the visual effect of the pattern itself, you might consider reading a sacred book or adding other visual aids into the process that also represent your goal. Returning to our illustration of the earth square again, a visual cue might translate into putting four potted plants, a globe, crystals, or other representatives of the earth's citizens at the four corners of the square. More simply, the words earth, air, fire, and water could be painted there as a reminder of the elements comprising creation.

By the way, don't overlook the potential of adding visualization when outward representations wouldn't be appropriate. For example, say you've prepared an amuletic maze to carry to work. It's often difficult in this environment to add sensory cues that won't disrupt the office or go against the rules. In this setting a visualization can fill in at least part of the gap by letting you see inwardly what doesn't exist without.

SOUND

Nearly all mystical traditions use sound as a sensory cue that heightens spiritual awareness. Be it a chant, mantra, sacred song, music, or prayer, each of these in some way stresses our partnership with the god/dess as their vibrations shift the energies all around. Better still, I have it on good authority that the god/dess doesn't care if you sing out of tune, if your voice cracks or wavers, or if you forget the words! The act of participating is more important than specifics—the way it makes you feel, the power it evokes, and eventually the results it achieves!

Another good alternative here is playing a suitably themed New Age/magickal CD or tape that inspires you. Or if you play a musical instrument, this could also become part of the labyrinth-walking exercises. Drums in particular seem to mingle well with a wide variety of patterns because you can change the rhythm to match your goal. Returning again to our earth-centered example, the four-four beat is ideal.

TASTE

This sensual cue is a little more difficult to bring into labyrinth walking, especially if you've been fasting. What I suggest as a compromise is a flavored beverage whose ingredients mirror your goal. For example, if you're designing a pattern to lift your spirits you might drink a berry juice, since berries are associated with abundant happiness. Take a sip just before designing your pattern or doing the exercise so that the taste lingers on your tongue. Also, some of the remainder can be poured out as a libation/offering that blesses and energizes your magick further.

TEXTURES

Add texture to your labyrinth-walking activities through what you wear or the fabric you use in creating large walkable patterns. In the first instance you're literally surrounding yourself with sympathetic vibrations. In the second, your feet or hands have direct contact with the texture so as to communicate the theme of your magick with each step you take.

Applied Patterning

The concepts of labyrinth walking won't be very useful to you if they just sit on a mental shelf somewhere collecting dust. You need to apply them so the patterns can start manifesting. So the next question facing prospective labyrinth walkers is, How? How do we put these patterns to use in our magick and our daily lives? This section will help you answer that question.

As you read it, bear in mind that you need not use all these methods. Instead, use only those that (a) have personal meaning, (b) make sense considering your goal, and (c) help you shift your awareness to a higher spiritual level so that your mind and soul can work cooperatively with the pattern to create the desired energy.

Dancing the Pattern

Life is movement, and historically speaking many labyrinth-styled patterns were used as part of sacred dancing to accentuate that movement. The Israelites danced in patterned processionals before the Ark of the Covenant. Tribal shamans danced to make the corn grow or to propitiate specific elemental beings. In Oceanic cultures dance was a way to tell the stories of the gods, and recount histories.

Why all this dancing? Because the ancients believed, and I think rightly so, that dance rejoices the human and divine spirit. It brings one's body into the act of worship and communion, and as we release ourselves to the dance our emotions also join in, followed by our very souls.

Five Hints for Sacred Labyrinth Dancing

1. Go to where you want to start the pattern wearing comfortable shoes or no shoes at all. Stretch a bit and shake the tension out of your arms.

2. Take three deep, cleansing breaths, then look at the pattern stretched out before you. Does it have a rhythm and cadence all its own? Listen to that energy with your spiritual ears. Continue breathing deeply so you're in a meditative frame of mind.

3. When you feel ready, start to sway to the sound of the energy pattern that crackles in the air all around. If it helps, try to trace the pattern in the air with your hands like an elaborate pantomime that grows as you get more of your body involved.

4. Release yourself to the pattern and the active principle of movement. You've been moving since before the day you were born. Feel the magick in it—in the way your heart beats with a drum that calls to you, to the center of the labyrinth.

5. Dance! Continue until you feel yourself naturally slowing down, then sit and make notes of your experience.

Since the goal of labyrinth walking is to experience all aspects of self and the divine wholly (the active principle), dancing the sacred path can lead us to that goal.   For those of you with two left feet, don't despair! Thankfully there are no real rules about what form labyrinth dancing should take. Some people just stand at the edge or center of their pattern and sway. Others put on music and really let loose. Others still make every step a pattern on the pattern as a way of doubling the symbolic value of the activity.

What's most important here is how you feel when you're dancing: what it makes you aware of, what insights come to you through the movements. If you feel awkward and insecure, and don't really release yourself to the pattern, the activity will likely fall flat. When you get so caught up in how you're working magick rather than the "whys" of it, you're in the wrong place! Remember, for the most part labyrinth walking is a solitary experience. You need not impress anyone with fancy footwork. Just do what comes naturally and make sure you give yourself enough room so that when inspiration hits you won't be falling over anything.

Dreaming the Pattern

Psychological studies seem to confirm that our subconscious and superconscious self can communicate with us more effectively during our sleeping hours. More than likely this is because it's the only time we slow down enough to really listen. Many people have also found that listening to language or subliminal instruction tapes as they sleep improves learning and helps with habit-changing. With this in mind, labyrinth walking could become a medium for inspiring insightful dreams or act as a way of growing spiritually even when we're asleep.

How you go about this depends on you, but here are some ideas to get you started.

1. Find a pattern that represents the energy you want to create. Look at that pattern just before you go to sleep. Observe long enough that you can see it clearly in your mind's eye with your physical eyes closed. When you lay down, breathe deeply and continue seeing that pattern until you fall naturally asleep. Repeat this over several nights if the first attempt isn't successful. Make notes of your experiences.

2. Put a pattern or patterns around your bed or under your pillow before going to sleep (if you can find them, wear pj's with the right patten on them). You will know those designs are there, saturating the room with the vibrations you need. Keep sleeping surrounded in magick until the energy has manifested substantially in your waking hours.

3. Memorize a labyrinth pattern (simple), then build it in your mind like a hedge maze. As you go to sleep, begin mentally making your way through the maze toward your goal. Some people find this activity continues in the dream scape!

4. Tape record a labyrinth-walking activity leaving pauses periodically on the tape so you can create the vision in your mind (note: people who have trouble remembering detailed designs will find this approach a lot easier than numbers 1 or 3). Keep listening and visualizing until you fall asleep and see what dreams may come!

Note that to any one of these techniques you could add other sensual cues like specifically textured blankets, burning a stick of incense in a fire-safe container, and playing sacred music in the background.

Pathworking Patterns

Pathworking is a kind of meditative exercise in which a person is led through a series of visualizations. At specific points along the way, the individual becomes a map maker for the activity by answering riddles, overcoming challenges, and/or choosing between several options presented. This makes pathworking a kind of labyrinth-walking exercise already, so adding extra maze or mandala-styled patterns into the process won't be difficult.

In this case the individuals undertaking the pathworking should look through various patterns and determine which ones might help them reach their goal. Then whoever guides them through the pathworking can integrate that pattern into the visualization in any way suited to the astral landscape being created. For example, a pathworking that's mentally set in a natural location could easily have a hedge maze as part of it, whereas one that takes place in an indoor setting might include a labyrinth painting on one of the described walls. Since both these patterns are going to be created in the participant's mind anyway, the imagery they devise will be wholly right for them. In other words, your mind won't conjure up a visualization to which it cannot relate and integrate into the overall experience.

I also highly recommend adding incense and music that accent the surroundings of the astral landscape. Returning to our outdoor example, pine might be one choice for an aromatic that engenders a stronger connection to a forest. Then adding a nature CD with birds chirping rounds out the sensual imagery. You should be aware that sounds and aromas have patterns too! So their design connects with the labyrinth and becomes part of it, making a multi-dimensional experience that's bound to improve the results.

Making Amuletic Patterns

Historical labyrinths were always made in gardens or built out of stones. Some maze, mandala, and labyrinth motifs were carved on buildings, made into jewelry, or placed on other objects to protect that item, its bearer, or an area from evil spirits. The reason for this choice of designs comes from the old superstition that evil spirits can't go around corners, which is something that all of these patterns have plenty of!

Another use for these smaller versions of the labyrinth was to turn back storms, which were often considered the embodiment of an angry spirit! This example makes me think about the intricately patterned sand paintings of the Navaho that turn back the spirit of sickness. The application seems very similar, yet they appear half a world apart from one another.

Bearing the continuity of these traditional applications in mind, it seems to me that labyrinth-styled patterns make an excellent medium for amulets, which have a preventative nature. Specifically, I'd recommend making portable patterns to turn back evil intention, banish negativity, safeguard yourself from ghosts, and similar protective goals. For durability, try carving your pattern on a wood slice, painting a piece of cloth, drawing it on paper and treating it with art spray, or using another medium that's easily carried. This way you can literally take your magickal patterns and the energy they bear with you everywhere to reach out beyond the self and re-design life's tapestry.

Many ancient amulets were created in astrological times, like a waning moon so troubles would "shrink," or a waxing moon to draw blessings in place of the negativity. Mages also often used valuable materials, or those that had sympathy with the magick being created through the design. So, when circumstances allow, you may want to consider following these two historical guidelines for two very good reasons.

First, propitious timing and sympathetic materials both provide extra support for your labyrinth-walking exercise. If you think of how important timing and physical condition is to conception, the idea is similar except the "baby" you're conceiving is power. When the timing is right on, when the "materials" are right, fertility is abundant, and therefore the results improve. The same holds true for your magick.

Second, time (read: hours, days, months, seasons, years) and sympathetic energy matrices are two other labyrinth-types that you can explore singularly or in tandem with other magickal methods. Both these things have built-in patterns that humans cannot "break," but there's no rule that says we can't build on them to make the most of the foundational blueprint we've been given!

Patterned Spells and Rituals

Spells and rituals both carry patterns that can be accentuated by adding labyrinths into the process. With spell work, you can use your body to make a pattern in the air while casting. You can also use components that bear suitable patterns (sensually or by their associated metaphysical correspondence), or you can pattern the way you put the elements of the spell together for specific outcomes.

To illustrate: a love spell might be designed so that the components are released to a southerly wind (emotional warmth) in a specific order. The order chosen directly relates to the component's symbolic value. For example, in this case a pinch of lemon powder might go first to promote friendship, followed by lavender for harmony and joy, followed by rose petals for love. This way the entire process builds in much the same way as most relationships form, matching the pattern desired.

The power of patterns becomes even more clear when one observes magickal rituals. It's very interesting to note that ancient mages often physically drew a magick circle (a mandala) on the floor before enacting any type of ritual. Similarly, pagan tradition in Scandinavia calls for a couple to come to the center of a circle to begin their life together. In both cases, the circle holds tremendous symbolism: the end and a beginning; time and not time; protection and empowerment; the within and without. I personally believe that the circle is one of the most important patterns of power that we'll discuss in this book, but let's return to rituals specifically.

Magickal ritual also illustrates square or cross motifs when the practitioner calls on the four watchtowers (the winds or elements) to watch and guide the proceedings. Rituals honor the sun's patterns when the practitioner moves clockwise through the sacred space to build positive energy, or counterclockwise to banish unwanted influences. Ritual effectively patterns a cone of power from the will of the witch, sometimes by inscribing sigils in the air, sometimes through dance, and sometimes by chanting or spellcraft. And better still, by nature a ritual's successful patterns are repeated not just once, but over generations!

Personal History Patterns

I want you to consider getting yourself a small bound book with blank, unlined pages. As important events occur in your life (like the birth of a child, changing jobs, graduation, and moving to a new residence), take a moment to make a pattern of that experience in this unique journal. Why? Because that pattern will communicate an awful lot about how you really feel at this moment, about the person you're becoming, and about the prevalent energies in your life.

Say, for example, someone decides to end an unproductive relationship. When they sit down and create a mandala-styled drawing of this situation, it comes out as having two distinct halves, one of which is dark and the other is bright, and a lot of little dots and squiggles outside the main pattern. The interpretive value of the two halves is obvious from the separation, but the colors and doodles are another matter. This individual now needs to examine themselves to determine if he or she perceives him- or herself as the negative factor in this relationship. He or she also needs to consider whether outside influences added unhealthy stress and pressure to the relationship. Answering those two questions will prove vital in the healing process ahead.

Another good example can be seen in making a career change. This individual decides to apply the skills in a new way. This is depicted on paper as a path that suddenly splits. One path just disappears off the paper, while the other continues to a door that's still closed. This labyrinth-styled drawing indicates that the person in question isn't sure what would have happened to them if they continued along the path they were already on. It also reveals that they're not wholly certain about how this change is going to affect the future (the closed door).

From these two examples I think you can see how historical patterning can give you a lot of perspective with which to work. This application is just like any other given herein, so make sure you're in the right frame of mind to give it a try, and that you have a variety of colors from which to create your pattern. If you want, tie this activity into the next application, that of making a labyrinth-walking diary.

A Labyrinth-Walking Diary

One of the greatest gifts you can give yourself is a written, typed, or tape-recorded rendition of your magickal experiences. Labyrinth walking is no exception, and keeping a diary offers many advantages. For one, each time you try a pattern and apply it to your life you'll likely experience various levels of failure and success. Noting these will help you better plan your designs in the future.

Second, keeping a record like this allows you to share ideas with other people who might not have normally thought of the pattern you created (and who might also find it very fulfilling). Third, and perhaps most importantly, this diary reveals your progress as a spiritual person. If you read it over several times a year I'm willing to bet you'll find an amazing change in the way you perceive things—because perception is part of the transformational pattern process!

Memorizing Patterns

As you discover key patterns that have a profound impact on your psyche and day-to-day reality, commit a few of them to memory. That way, when you need a labyrinth's influence to manifest, or want to support the patterns you're trying to integrate, you can develop the appropriate images in your imagination. When done mindfully and regularly, hate and intolerance can be eclipsed by a portrait of love and acceptance; a world of chaos and noise with a picture of order and inner quiet. Your entire mental landscape can begin to take on a positive pattern that cannot help but slowly leak into daily life.

In many ways you'll find that life itself is a sacred pattern and everything else we add to that pattern with thoughtfulness becomes like icing on the cake. It will make your reality into an ongoing labyrinth where you're slowly, but surely moving toward the center, toward the Sacred, and toward the magick that's already part of your soul.

Food for Thought

Before moving on to looking at labyrinths, mazes, and mandalas individually, I'd like to share a few last collective insights for your consideration:

- Bear in mind that the linguistics of sacred patterns have often been blurred in historical writings, so it really doesn't matter what you call the pattern—what matters is its meaningfulness to you and the power it evokes when you use it.

- The phrase "I am the way" is very important to your exploration of labyrinth walking. The words "I am" speak of your realness, your presence, and your connection with the life's network. It also speaks of the greatness of the Sacred Parent.

In walking any path or using any sacred pattern, you are following the "way" back to oneness with self, others, the earth, and the god/dess in your soul.

- Among the Hopis, Cretans, and other mystical groups, the earth's womb holds a special pattern. When a person's spirit enters this pattern they leave reborn (specifically on a psychic level). With this in mind, nature's sacred patterns represent a potent tool for reactivating human spiritually and our associated psychic powers.

Finally, in many esoteric traditions, one could not enter a labyrinth without being initiated. So the process of studying and using sacred patterns represents a very important spiritual genesis, if you'll allow it to be so. Each time you open yourself to the possibilities and potential of a pattern, and allow the associated energy to transform your spirit, you have taken another step forward toward magickal adeptness, toward wholeness, and toward that seemingly elusive quality called enlightenment.

Labyrinth in Ely Cathedral, 1870

2

LABYRINTHS: BEAUTY'S BLUEPRINT

To turn, turn will be our delight, till by turning, turning we become right.

—Shaker hymn

The migration of whales is a labyrinth pattern. The annual hibernation of bears is a labyrinth pattern. The blood in motion and our very breath is a kind of labyrinth. In fact, all things in life are part of creation's labyrinth. This is a truth that magickal practitioners recognize and work with regularly.

Be it the eleventh-century Amiens Cathedral in France or the Angel's Nest Labyrinth built in modern times, there is a mystery and amazement surrounding labyrinths that's hard to escape no matter your spiritual tradition. Of all enigmatic patterns, the labyrinth stands out as being among the most widely studied. Be it laid out in water-worn stone, the floor of a church, or in living turf, the importance of the labyrinth's pattern is also illustrated by its alternative title: the Mandala of European and Mediterranean cultures. How did it get this title?

Consider first the labyrinth's design. By definition, a labyrinth consists of a unicursal path that moves toward the center of a circle, not always directly, and back out again. The circle is like the border of the mandala, and the center equates to the point. Even so, as a whole pattern the finished effect is quite different. Rather than a symmetrical image that draws your attention to a specific spot, the labyrinth plays a bit with perspectives. The path twists and turns, in and out, before the seeker reaches the goal.

What symbolic purpose would be served by having a path that will always reach its designation, but only after some serious detours?   That question has laid heavy on many philosopher's minds, and it is one worthy of your meditations. The common answer is that the labyrinth is an analogy of life's pilgrimage. In essence, all of life is but one path where what we see depends on where one is standing! When we stop to look around that's when we discover, or perhaps remember, who we truly are in the greater scheme of things.

Since life's quest is rarely linear, the labyrinth meanders. If we continue along life's (and the labyrinth's) path in diligence, we will eventually find our way. But, even when we get "lost" the labyrinth's roadway can become a guide, directing us back into communion with the Sacred and our own souls. In this case all roads do, indeed, lead home!

But as you've probably already guessed, the symbolism doesn't end there. If you look at the ancient labyrinths, their paths are two-edged, representing dichotomies. More importantly, however, these borders create the perfect channel for energy. When a person or group stands at the beginning of a labyrinth-walking activity, their singular or communal energy precedes them down the proverbial walkway—it moves ahead of the pattern. In this manner the labyrinth can literally channel off negativity, and/or prepare the way ahead with sacredness and magick, never taking a wrong turn and never veering from the goal. Like a metaphorical riverbed, if the first path isn't right for this spiritual water, the energy will find another suitable way through the wilderness. This flow guides the seeker, even when his or her footing seems unsure, to the center of self, Spirit, and the heart of the labyrinth.

As you consider creating your own labryinth-walking activities, and review the examples later in this chapter, keep this flow in mind. Find or design a pattern that reaches a central symbolic point after some detours, then continue the pattern back out again so that "emergence" in a spiritual sense occurs. Remember that the process of making and using the labryinth is equally important (the process is a pattern too), something that the myths of the labryinth reveal.

The Labyrinth in Myth

One story of the labyrinth originates in a Swedish tale. It begins with a nasty troll (is there any other kind?) who captures a young girl and takes her to his labyrinth. People gathered outside the stronghold to try to rescue the lass, walking seven times back and forth until they gained entry. There they waited until the beast fell asleep, and they brought the girl out safely. There is strong evidence that connects this story with the annual cycle of the sun, the girl being a goddess type who is "rescued" from winter's darkness.

The second, and most widely known story about the labyrinth comes to us from Greece. I was personally very pleased about this happenstance. I feel that the Greeks had some of the best myths for illustrating the diversity of the human and divine nature (often in humorous ways). This story is no exception. In fact, the symbolism in this particular myth and its popularity throughout the world have effected labyrinth studies and theories for thousands of years.

We begin our tale with a man named Minos, the King of Crete who was also the son of Zeus. Minos was married to Pasiphae, who was also the daughter of a god, Helios. Now, if

Greek stories hold true to form, with all those gods and godlings involved you know there's bound to be trouble. Sure enough, there was.

It seems Minos had promised Poseidon an offering of a specific white bull, but gave another one instead. Poseidon felt this was a breach of faith, and caused Pasiphae to lust after the original white bull in an effort to humiliate Minos. The child of Pasiphae's union with the white bull was the man-bull known as the Minotaur or Asterius. This creature was so huge and monstrous that a special prison had to be built to contain it. As a side note, bulls in this region were often part of fertility rites, so I wonder if there was additional symbolic value here to people of the time—specifically the wisdom of "constraining" unnatural passions.

One of the most brilliant builders of the day, Daedalus, was given the unenviable task of contriving a suitable prison for the Minotaur. He then went on to create a three-dimensional housing, the Asterius—a very difficult labyrinth. His architectural feat was so impressive and difficult, in fact, that some students believe it may have actually been a maze! In either case, the labyrinth-maze was successful in housing the Minotaur. But this story, like most Greek tales, doesn't tie up loose ends that neatly.

Next we come to three other characters in the plot. The first is Androgeos, the son of Minos who died at the hand of an Athenian king. For this crime, Minos declared that Athenian children would be sacrificed to the Minotaur on a regular basis. This went on for many years until Minos' daughter, Ariadne, fell in love with an Athenian named Theseus. Theseus arranged to become the Minotaur's offering one year, then aided by his beloved overcame a hideous fate (namely becoming a snack food). As Virgil says:

> Here was seen the Labyrinth's web, in which the path
> was inextricably snarled, yet on Ariadne's great love Daeda-
> lus took pity; thus himself he solved the structure's tangled
> puzzle paths and led the blind step on the yarn.

Ariadne fastened a length of thread or yarn to Theseus so he could follow it back to her after his battle. What exactly transpired inside the labyrinth has been the subject of much conjecture. We're told Theseus slew the Minotaur, which sounds all too easy, but it makes for a great story. So, Theseus returns out of the labyrinth safe and whole, guided by the thread, and sacrifices to the Minotaur ended. In this manner Theseus fulfilled the role of the hero who arrives home from a monstrous undertaking with a great prize—in this case the "treasure" was the lives of innocent children.

The Athenians, being truly grateful (and being ones never to overlook a good occasion for a party), celebrated the miraculous news with a labryinthian-styled dance. To understand this, realize that dancing was very important to Greek rituals in that it invoked, honored, and thanked the sacred powers. It's notable that some labyrinths are still danced to this day, believing that this act releases the pattern's power!

But I'm getting away from the story, which hasn't ended yet. With Minos' power over Athens now defeated, he had to vent his anger somewhere—and poor Daedalus became the focus of it (here begins Daedalus' process). He and his son, Icarus, were banished to the Labyrinth. This was not about to daunt a builder like Daedalus, though. Rather than give himself over to defeat, he challenged the labyrinth, himself, linear thinking, and even the gods by making two pairs of wings from feathers, thread, and wax.

When the wings were completed, Daedalus cautioned his son not to fly so high as to melt the wax, nor so low as to dampen the feathers on the sea (a good example of the boundaries we all set for ourselves and others, and the two-edged nature of the labyrinth). Sadly, Icarus became overly enthusiastic and, dreaming of greatness, flew too high. He did not survive the attempt. This seems a very unfair ending for our hero, to lose his son at the moment of victory. What we don't know up to this point is that Daedalus was once from Athens himself. There he killed a young student whose brilliance surpassed Daedalus' own. So, the labyrinth had now become a karmic instrument. Besides, the story still isn't over!

After reasoning that his son's reckless, idealistic nature became his own undoing, Daedalus reconciled himself to Icarus' death and flew on to the region of Naples. There he built a temple to Apollo depicting the story of the labyrinth on it. He also went to Sicily and fashioned jewelry and buildings there. As Daedalus traveled, Minos continued the frustrating search for him. Alas, on finally discovering Daedalus, Minos fell prey to the Sicilian King's daughter who did not wish to let the master craftsman go elsewhere. She doused the King with pitch, which black color matched Minos' dark rage!

From this point forward we hear nothing more of Daedalus. Perhaps he lived out his life quietly, performing the skills for which he was most suited. Not the life of a hero, nor that of a father, but a simple builder whose path had led him back home.

By the way, the actual location of this famous labyrinth has historians and archaeologists alike scratching their heads. Some feel it was really part of the Knossos palace and the rest of the tale can be attributed to mythic elaboration. Others feel that it was hidden or completely destroyed by an earthquake in 1600 B.C.E. In either case, nothing that resembles this particular labyrinth has been uncovered in the region of Knossos yet.

As a second interesting postscript to this ancient tale, the path through the labyrinth is often called Ariadne's Thread. Her bundle of yarn was also sometimes referred to as a clew (modern spelling: clue), which gives whole new meaning to contemporary phrases such as "get a clue." It seems that, like Theseus, we're still trying to unravel the mysteries of our personal and planetary labyrinth!

The Winding Path

A writer and researcher by the name of Mircea Eliade said "the supreme rite of initiation is to enter the labyrinth and return from it, and yet every life, even the least eventful, can be taken as the journey through the labyrinth. The sufferings and trials undergone by Ulysses were fabulous, and yet any man's return home has the value of Ulysses' return to Ithaca." This quote rings very true for people in the magickal community.

For Wiccans, Pagans, Neo-Pagans, and those of similar metaphysical callings, the labyrinth has become a symbol of the Path of Beauty—our chosen walk in this life. While situations can deceive us, making us feel like we're getting nowhere (a theme common to many quest myths), the Path of Beauty will not lead us astray if we walk in diligence, truth, and love. The key here is knowing ourselves and trusting our magick enough to realize that transformation isn't in what "seems" to be. It's not cosmetic nor instantaneous. The effects of the labyrinth are also like that.

While inside the labyrinth, its course is the main source of our perspectives. Just as you think you can see the center, it moves you away from it again (just as when you think you have it together spiritually, and the proverbial rug gets pulled out from under you). At first this can discourage, but eventually the seeker catches on. They begin to see that shifts forward and backward are all part of the master plan, of the learning process. As long as we keep moving, keep putting one foot in front of the other, we remain a co-creator in that process. We become Ariadne's Thread, and like Ulysses we will get home!

The labyrinth's ability to help a person recognize true change, and its direct correlation to the initiation process, is likely why this pattern appeared as part of some European initiation rites among pagans and witches. At the outset of the ritual, an initiate was taken to the entryway of the labyrinth. While an adept was often waiting nearby in case an initiate lost their sense of direction, this individual was more than a guide. S/he guarded the Path, watching each person's responses to the labyrinth's energies closely.

The labyrinth's pattern was meant, in this case, to discourage and/or diligently challenge those seekers whose motivations might be askew. Even as Theseus faced a mock death in his labyrinth—a place of hidden terrors and truths, and of facing the self—the seeker on a metaphysical path must be wholly certain of his or her choice. They must be devoted and not merely curious. For those who had the right mind and heart, the design heightened the magick being created, and provided a sacred ambiance suited to such an important decision in any person's life. It then offered its path as the channel for that positive energy.

A Labyrinthian Dedication Rite

Those people reading this who would like to use the labyrinth as part of a solitary or group initiation may do so. Your labyrinth's path need not be complicated, just long enough, and winding enough, to allow the seeker introspective time. Lay this pattern out through the rooms of a house, in a yard, or in a field so that it stretches some way before reaching the center where an altar will be ready and waiting. This represents the altar of our body, our mind, our heart, and spirit in physical form. The exact decorations, tools, etc. that are laid out on the altar can be chosen by a priest/ess or by the initiate for significance.

At the opening into the labyrinth a seeker should be challenged somehow. If you're working alone this challenge can come in the form of pictures and tokens from your past—things that have made you what you are today. Each of these images and trinkets is important, but you are also turning a corner now. Some of the past, the negative parts, should be left behind.

For readers who are working with a group, have a guardian waiting for you at the opening of a labyrinth who will challenge you with various questions. For example: What words do you bring with you to this sacred space? (Answer: perfect love and perfect trust.) Other questions might revolve around your motivations, challenge your level of magickal knowledge or proficiency, and inquire as to what you wish to leave behind as you start a new life.

From this point forward walk the path you've laid out slowly and thoughtfully. Consider what has brought you to this place, and where you hope to go afterward. As the path turns, think of magick spinning and turning around you and within you. Become one with that energy before you reach the center.

As you approach the altar, acknowledge whatever energies you perceive there, be it the elements, the Divine, or your higher self. From this point forward you must trust your instincts. If you feel guided to pray or meditate, do so. If you feel like laughing or crying, the same holds true. Only you can know what the self altar means in your life and your magick, and only you can receive its message on this day.

If you are working with a group you will likely receive some instructions at this juncture or participate in other activities. For example, in times past magickal groups were very secretive, so an initiate might have been asked to take a vow of silence about the identities of group members. The trust and mutual responsibility implied in such an act is obvious when you think of the witch hunts. People were quite literally entrusting their lives to each other. Today, this type of vow might translate into promising to help protect the integrity of your Path, and support the other members of your group.

The route back out of the labyrinth is one of rejoicing. Magickal dance is perfectly appropriate, as is skipping and other uplifting movements. Express how you feel physically even if you may not be able to do so verbally. Make notes of your experience in your magickal journal, and consider discussing it with other like-minded folk if you have any lingering questions.

Other esoteric traditions employed (and continue to use) the Labyrinths' symbolism too. In Cabalism, for example, the Tree of

Life is a labyrinthian image with eleven circuits. When a person follows this pattern it progresses him or her toward realizing true magick, responsibly and powerfully. Similarly, the Hopi shaman's medicine wheel (see previous activity) has four circuits designed to create wholeness in body and spirit. And while neither of these cultures called those patterns a "labyrinth" the similarities in purpose and energies are unmistakable.

This brings up an important point to remember throughout this book. Sacred patterns are often interrelated. The base geometrics find expression in every society, in culturally diverse ways. This means that a foundational matrix, like that of a labyrinth, can be recognized no matter its name. It's simply a matter of looking at the way each pattern is created and applied.

The Medicine Wheel

To make your own medicine wheel, begin much as you will for mandalas with an outer circle. Use a color that represents wholeness to you. Within this wheel draw a labyrinth that has four circuits (if you wish this can be two that go in and two that go out—this pattern emphasizes balance). Each of the four circuits should bear elemental colors: red for fire, yellow for air, blue for water, green for earth. As you color the circuits, you can invoke the elements so their energy resonates in your portable labyrinth. Here's one sample invocation:

Red: *Red around, turn, and bent*
             The fires burn; the magick's sent!

Yellow: *Yellow around, turn and leave*
             The wind rings out; in the magick believe!

Blue: *Blue around, turn, and glow*
             The waves roll in; the magick flows!

Green: *Green around, turn, and root*
             The earth's alive; magick's afoot!

Labyrinths in History

Like the mandala, the labyrinth has an old and rather illustrious history. It begins in Sardinia with a stone-carved labyrinth relief dating to about 2500 B.C.E. This is likely the oldest remaining image of a discernible labyrinth pattern. And from what we know of oral tradition and prehistories, this carving indicates that the labyrinth has been part of human consciousness for nearly five thousand years.

Moving forward in history a bit, the remains of an important labyrinth-patterned building is located in Fayum, Egypt. This edifice dates to about 1800 B.C.E., having been devised by Pharaoh Amenemhet III, who had it erected near his pyramid. This labyrinth had twelve covered courts, and upper and lower levels. The lower levels, however, were reserved as tombs for kings and sacred crocodiles. (In Egyptian myths, a crocodile god Seybek emerged from the waters after creation to organize the world.)

Both Strabo and Herodotus mentioned the elaborate nature of this labyrinth, the former of the two saying it was equal to the pyramids in grandeur. When you consider that this structure spanned 1,000 by 800 feet, its easy to see why these historians were impressed. Unfortunately the four thousand-year-old labyrinth was pretty well destroyed by the Romans. Even so, legend says that Amenemhet's labyrinth was the prototype that Daedalus used in designing his masterpiece!

Speaking of Daedalus, the Greek myth of the labyrinth first appears around the fifteenth century B.C.E. Shortly thereafter, archaeological remains from civilizations throughout Europe and the Mediterranean appear, including items like coins and pottery with labyrinth patterns on them. For example, one coin unearthed with the labyrinth pattern pressed into it dates to 1300 B.C.E., originating in Syria.

Another illustration is a clay tablet from the palace of Nestor (Pylos) dating from 1200 B.C.E. This has a doodle of a labyrinth on the reverse side. This particular find is indicative of how common the pattern had become by this early historical juncture, considering the front of the tablet contained the financial figures for a lucrative sheep transaction!

Despite its popularity, the word labyrinth wasn't coined until about 450 B.C.E. by historian Herodotus, just after the coins of Knossos also began showing the Minotaur and labyrinth pattern on them (500 B.C.E.). Mind you, this wasn't the only area where labyrinth patterns were appearing. Along the Baltic sea over six hundred stone labyrinths have been uncovered, probably having been constructed and used for luck in fishing or fertility rites.

The Labyrinth for Summerland or Safety

You can make special labyrinths for friends and loved ones who have passed over as a way of blessing their spirits and helping guide them to their next existence. Begin with a labyrinth pattern that you feel would appeal to the deceased. Put their photograph in the middle of it, or perhaps at the end of it (this symbolizes successful completion). Either burn this near the resting place of that individual to release the pattern's energy, or bury it with them if possible.

For personal blessings and protection you can make a similar labyrinth for yourself. Use a color for the Thread of Ariadne that you associate with safety and put your picture in the middle. Carry this with you regularly. If you ever experience an incident in which your safety is threatened but you come through it unscathed, you might want to burn or bury this and make a new one. The first has done its job!

There is some evidence suggesting that early labyrinths may have been partly associated with the cult of the dead. One in a Sardinian cave supports this theory by using a labyrinthian pattern to show the deceased spirit a route to follow after death, and the ultimate transformation of rebirth at the end. The fact that this particular image was deep within the Mother's womb is profound from a symbolic standpoint. It alludes to the labyrinth's feminine nature and connection with the archetypal goddess, in this case specifically those who oversee the underworld. It's an interesting bit of synchronicity that ancient miners in Spain carried similar images to the Sardinian one when they went down into the earth as protective charms!

A second plausible application for labyrinths was as a physical representation of sun's movement through the day and the year. The various paths may be symbolic of not only the earth's seasonal meter, but also of the ongoing rhythm of life, death, and rebirth (tying this function to the cult of the dead spoken of earlier). When the labyrinth was created or used for this purpose it was likely danced—the pathway becoming the sacred ground for the celebrants to joyfully follow.

A third application for labyrinths that is a historical certainty was that of hosting courting and wedding rites. In these rituals the labyrinthian pattern was often called a Virgin Dance, and rightly so. Popularized during the 1600s in Europe, but practiced long before then, love labyrinths were created specifically for the symbolism they evoked for both the participants and watchers. After all, the path of a happy marriage certainly twists and turns around a point!

Here's how the Virgin Dance rituals worked. Usually a young woman was placed in the center of these designs (symbolically safe) while a suitor (or sometimes two suitors) would try to reach her and bear her out, similar to the old bride captures and broomstick jumping of pagan and magickal traditions. Success in this endeavor represented a similar pairing, and the couple was then married.

A slight variation on this theme was to have a couple recite vows at the center of a labyrinth pattern, then emerge together to mark their new life. In both cases the woman takes the dramatic role of Ariadne to the hopeful Theseus, letting love lead the right man down the path.

Love's Labyrinth

You can make this as a nice gift item for newlyweds to help safeguard their relationship and keep love alive. Begin with three 6-foot lengths of cord: one red (for passion), one blue (for joy), and one white (for peace). Braid these together as you keep the couple in your thoughts. Each time the three cords cross, make a wish for the couple that seems appropriate. When the braid is complete lay it down on a wooden or other sturdy surface to which you can affix it securely. Make a labyrinth pattern the center of which is a heart. (If you want, put a picture of the couple inside the safety of that heart.) I suggest using a strong bonding agent to adhere this to your chosen surface so your labyrinth pattern doesn't symbolically begin to dissolve over time. Finally, hand paint the couple's names and the date of marriage on the exterior of the labyrinth so they can use it as a keepsake.

The protective, nurturing nature of the labyrinth revealed itself in other settings besides marriage rituals, however. It also emerged in architecture. Simple homes, seafaring ships, and great cathedrals alike often bore a labyrinthian carving or painting, usually over the front door or on a masthead, to keep all within safe.

Traditional labyrinths were made from many different materials including stone, dirt, flowers, or hedges. Sometimes also called a City of Turns, labyrinths were often built right into sacred sites. Some sites had the labyrinth near an entryway while others had them as an integral part of the site itself.

One example of the latter is Chartres Cathedral in France. Chartres is an excellent illustration of a Gothic labyrinth set into the middle of a glorious sanctuary. What's really interesting about this site is that it sets atop an area that has been regarded as a potent earth vortex for thousands of years. Druids gathered here to honor the goddess and Christians worshiped Mary here, so it's not surprising that a labyrinth developed on this site. The feminine energy is overwhelming.

Legends tell us that the Templar knights discovered the measures for the Cathedral at Solomon's Temple. The result is that the entire chamber that houses the labyrinth resonates with wakeful, watchful energy. Tradition dictates that this eleven-circuit labyrinth be walked barefoot to put the participant in direct contact with the pattern, the center of which lies directly over the vortex known to the Druids and early Christian teachers.

Across the ocean in the new world, the labyrinth appeared among Native Americans too. The Hopi drawings for mother and child, and that for Mother Earth, for example, bear unicursal imagery. Many Hopi ritual dances also take labyrinthian spiraling forms (inward to denote death or decrease, and outward for life and increase).

Similarly, the Iroquois and other Northeastern tribes use a double curve motif, but without any religious connotations that we can discern. Various other tribes also exhibit unicursal patterns most often bearing seven rings and four lines in the circumference. This isn't surprising since the numbers seven and four are sacred among many native peoples. What's really interesting here is that these images appear long before the Native Americans knew anything of European or Mediterranean labyrinths. Such likeness in patterns supports the idea of the labyrinth as a long-standing global archetype in human awareness.

With these magickal traditions and history in mind, labyrinth-walking activities can be designed for one of several spiritual purposes, including:

- Focusing on life at this moment, and understanding it better. This can be accomplished by honing in on the center of the labyrinth (your goal), its path (your life's path), or the borders (your taboos or limitations).

- Pondering a difficult situation or individual to discern the best way to proceed. In this case making the labyrinth in any form is simply a meditative tool that releases your mind to think more creatively.

- Asking a specific question and allowing the labyrinths pattern to respond. Here, you might begin with one basic pattern (a circle), but as you create it you allow the pattern to transform. Whatever it becomes is your answer in symbolic form.

- Interpreting the meaning in a dream or vision. Here you can use the labyrinth to "walk out" your dream, to draw it in symbolic form, or as a meditative focus that will help you replay the dream's details for better understanding.

- Opening the lines of communication with your own inner wisdom. This type of labyrinth activity is undertaken in silence. No matter the medium, you (and your environment) must be still for spirit and the higher self to speak.

- Breaking destructive tendencies in order to build anew. Here, a labyrinth might begin in completed form that represents the negative pattern. That pattern can be burned or buried, then you make a new one and keep it in a place of honor to mark your determined transition.

- Disconnecting from, or becoming less dependent upon, the mechanical in order to honor the natural. Here I suggest an outdoor labyrinth activity, especially a topiary-style labyrinth.

- Challenging preconceived notions versus Universal realities and truths. Your preconceived notions are patterns too. To break those or transform them takes time, but the path of the labyrinth provides guidance in accomplishing this goal. Here you might move through the first half of the creation process backward, then turn forward for the rest—symbolically turning things around.

- Stabilizing chaotic energy so that previously unrecognized options and possibilities come into focus. The channel of your labyrinth is sure. Whatever pathway you make in your pattern will let energy flow through. The straighter the path, the less confusing the result.

- Reestablishing the lines of communication with the god/dess, and then keeping those lines open afterward. Circular labyrinths or oval ones in particular seem to house strong goddess energy.

- Becoming aware of guardian angels and spirit guides. Many people report meeting spirits during their labyrinth activities. This pattern of power seems to welcome their presence and interaction.

- Learning to coordinate body, mind, and spirit into a unified whole moving toward a goal. You cannot simply make a labyrinth—you must experience it.

- Inspiring creativity or overcoming artistic blockages. Again this has to do with the labyrinth's path as a channel way. Open the door on the side of the labyrinth that represents self, then let the energy flow through the design you've created for it.

- Releasing emotional obstructions or suspending old patterns and making new ones with all due sensitivity.

- Creating protective, defensive, walls for fortifying energy (the walls of the labyrinth).

- Blending thought with feeling and action, or the ego with spirit. Again this takes us back to the idea that labyrinth walking is not simply a physical activity or craft but a conscious blend of body-mind-spirit moving together toward one goal through that activity or craft.

- Encouraging a sense of community for a group. Moving an entire group through a labyrinth activity toward a center point helps unite them in spirit and purpose.

- Honoring the past to understand the present and build a better future (the path into and out of the labyrinth).

Bear in mind that chapter 1 discusses the many forms that your labyrinth activities can take. It's up to you to decide which medium and approach is best considering your goals.

Overall, the labyrinth represents one means of rediscovering and defining the meaning, purpose, challenges, guidance, and motivation for living by metaphysical ideology. The meaning of the Path is determined by the individual walking it, as is the purpose. Our challenge is to take off mundane veils and look at the invisible binding ties to all things. The guidance offered by the labyrinth is to move past the physical toward our inner sacred space. Finally, the motivation is enlightenment and reunion with the Divine, nothing more and nothing less.

A Modern Rebirth

It is no coincidence that the labyrinth's path is sometimes called the Road to the New Jerusalem. For many modern seekers it has come to represent that kind of spiritual quest and awakening—the awakening that's been happening since long before the misnomer "New Age" came into the public eye. Trust me when I say that nothing we've experienced in New Age ideology is "new"!

There exists a growing awareness that the labyrinth is a spiritual tool that can be used by any seeker, no matter their religion. In response to this awareness (or perhaps more correctly as a confirmation of it), hedge-, floor-, and wall-styled labyrinths are sprouting all over the world, watered by an esoteric swell. These beautiful, insightful achievements will stand for a very long time as an expression of humankind's communal recognition that something's been missing in our lives. They will stand as a testament to our spiritual rebirth.

In modern applications, the labyrinth's symbolic value hasn't changed much. Even so, there are some things about this symbolism that bears thoughtful reflection in an updated context. In considering our times, the path toward the center of the labyrinth can symbolize what we need to lose, give up, or forgive. In our very material world, filled with anger and discord, this path is hard for many people to traverse. Note that I said hard, *not* impossible. The difference lies within the seeker's determination.

The center of the labyrinth represents each individual in the best, purest form possible. With so much apathy and insecurity in our children, one can easily see the importance of this "point." Once a person reaches the labyrinth's central sacred space with an open mind and heart, it can dissolve the unhealthy perceptions that society, environment, and experience may have instilled in the questor (and by extension, all of humanity). Again, no easy task. It requires that we strip away layers and layers of well-rehearsed rhetoric and bare ourselves to the truth—the mirror in the center of our labyrinth—the very nucleus of our soul.

The path out of the labyrinth has two major functions: balancing and internalizing whatever the inbound path brought to light. In so doing, this part of the exercise becomes an active illustration of what the questor found, healed, or recognized;

again, three things very important to our times. So many of us are seeking something that we can't quite explain. Others are hurting and confused. Many others still don't care anymore, feeling wholly lost in the Shakespearian "petty pace" of daily life.

In answer to this ongoing human struggle, the triune-teaching of the labyrinth's inbound thread (lose, relinquish, forgive) and outbound thread (find, heal, recognize) is as sure as the ancient goddess herself. The maiden releases us. She encourages the act of discovery and renews our zeal for life. The mother awaits our burdens with open arms in the center of the labyrinth. There she will hold us close and tend our wounds. The crone guides us the rest of the way using wisdom and discernment as a beacon.

In the end, the questor claims and carries whatever was discovered at the labyrinth's core into the world, and then blesses others with it. The entire process is an archetype for tapping into, and potentially bettering, the human collective unconscious as described by Carl Jung. Thus, the labyrinth gives us a complete cycle that ends in closure, clarity, and wholeness. What a tremendous gift for a busy and often chaotic era!

If you have the chance to visit a pre-existing labyrinth and walk it (see chapter 6), you will find that beyond these gifts the labyrinth also poses questions like its cousin the mandala. Even if you can't travel to these sights, you can trace the patterns with your finger instead. In either case, after you walk or work the pattern you will want to consider:

- Did you stay on course or find your own way? Sometimes the labyrinth calls to us to live between the lines, and other times to exceed them.

- What about the symbolic language of the labyrinth did you find most powerful and touching? This language can (and will) nourish your soul if you can learn to recognize it, and then truly connect with what it's saying to you.

- What was the central dynamic of your experience: physical, emotional, mental, or spiritual? Each is important, but most labyrinth-walking activities center around one of these that answers a need, or refines and aids a goal.

Finally, if you could have played any type of music during your experience, what would it have been and why? The labyrinth tends to strike a chord within us. It's as if by following the path we are also following in the footsteps of a great conductor. The score here is an ancient song in which each of us sings one part. Find the song, and you find yourself. Find the conductor and you find God.

Deconstructing the Labyrinth

As a brief review, the traditional labyrinth has no intersections. The path continually shifts directions going past the center point repeatedly, and completely fills the interior space with circuits. This very same course provides one route in and back out of the center point. Additionally, a large number of ancient labyrinths have seven or eleven circuits, but there are certainly variations on this theme.

Labyrinths are designed for active energy. Neither the Sacred nor life is static. By embarking on the labyrinth you awaken this active energy and accept it as a road map for the intuitive nature (a maze, by comparison, works on the rational levels). Even with this knowledge, however, there are many subtle signals in the labyrinth's construction of which you should be aware in designing your own labyrinth-walking activities.

We have already discussed the path of the labyrinth partially. In Labyrinth terminology it's often called Ariadne's Thread. Thesus never needed Ariadne's tether; it was her love that was the guiding, motivating force on his adventure. The path was always there and always sure—it is only the perception of the path that changes. So it is that the path equates to individualization and ultimate self-realization where the center is the "point." With this in mind, the labyrinth might be considered a twin, open-ended mandala! Even so, the path is only one part of the sacred pattern.

Most labyrinths are enclosed within a circle, and have symmetrical layouts also like the mandala. This circle bears consideration in that it points to important aspects of our daily reality. For example, what circles do we travel in life? Who is part of our extended tribal circle—our friends, acquaintances, and family members? In what circles do we work and play? Are we literally going around in circles in terms of our spiritual pursuits? More importantly, how fares our soul in the circle of the mundane world?

There are other symbolic parts to the labyrinth as well. An angle along the path represents unknown things, and our perspectives about those things. The labyrs (a double-axe image that is visible at the labyrinth's turns) is an emblem of the goddess, the feminine force behind life's spark. This reiterates the labyrinth's overall feminine design.

The center of the labyrinth, perhaps the most important part, is called a rosette. Historians believed this is yet another symbol of the Mother of all things. And, just as a rose is a cosmic wheel in miniature, the center of the labyrinth is a perfect mandala representing the ability of each individual to achieve enlightenment (or anything else for which they may be striving). At this timeless point reason meets imagination, the empirical meets the mystical, and dogmatic suffocation is transformed into spiritual liberation.

Here are some other patterns that are important to traditional labyrinth designs and their meanings:

Colors

I have not found any study of the labyrinth that discusses the colors used for their symbolic value. This may be for one of two theoretical reasons. First, the colors may have been chosen pragmatically rather than intuitively. After all, hedge labyrinths (for example) don't give you a lot of variety of hue from which to choose. Second, the color values may have been so traditional that the makers and subsequent students of the labyrinth simply took them for granted.

Whichever theory you personally ascribe to doesn't really matter. Go with what's sensible or what's spiritually pleasing. Both are perfectly appropriate!

Patterns

As you might expect, the labyrinth doesn't have quite as much written about its various patterns simply because it didn't use nearly as many as mandalas did. That doesn't mean you can't expand on this list for yourself using personally meaningful adaptations. It just means that this selection of resource information is a little scant! Here are some of the patterns we find repeatedly mentioned and their symbolic value. Consider these when you're designing your labyrinth activities:

- **Braided edges:** Ariadne's Thread of love that encompasses the seeker and keeps him/her safe
- **Circle:** unity; surrendering to wholeness
- **Concentric rings:** time and space, and often the seeker's place in either
- **Concentric squares:** healing; this also might be suitable as a charm for financial stability
- **Inward turning spiral:** creating the vortex or cone of power; generative force
- **Line (the path):** life's journey; unfolding creation
- **Outward-turning spiral:** integration and empowerment; unwinding the magick; manifestation
- **Web:** life's network, within and without

Turns

The turns a labyrinth makes symbolize change. It also represents our spirit's slow, but steady, evolution.

- **Three turns:** heaven; celestial matters; universal consciousness
- **Four turns:** earth; temporal matters; tribal consciousness
- **Seven turns:** healing (often physical); reconciliation; spiritual progress; rites of passage
- **Eleven turns:** inner mysteries; emotions; psychism and mysticism; life's journey; salvation; order; ritual
- **Twelve turns:** magick; the meeting ground between the Sacred and humankind; communion
- **Thirteen turns:** Christ consciousness; awakening the lunar, intuitive self

The modern rebirth of the interest in labyrinth building has brought with it a lot of variations on the traditional motif. Some labyrinths, like that of Daedalus' making, are very complex with symbolic patterns suited to their location or application. Others have maintained a more ancient appeal. In considering the archetypes to which humankind responds, neither of these approaches is right or wrong. What matters is the results they achieve. So it is too with your own labyrinth-walking creations.

Walking the Labyrinth

In reading about various people's labyrinth-walking experiences, one thing came into vivid view. The whole process is very much like a pilgrimage. It begins with but one bold step, moves through fears, doubts, and challenges, and ends with acceptance and liberation. You will see facets of these phases in every labyrinth-walking activity you undertake, just manifested slightly differently depending on your chosen media, applications, personal needs, and ultimate goals.

No matter your purpose, however, you can follow these basic steps for any labyrinth-walking activities to make this experience as positive and powerful as possible:

1. Consider if you want to fast, pray, or meditate for a predetermined period of time beforehand so you're wholly prepared for the experience.

2. Remove your watch. Many people indicate a feeling of timelessness when walking the labyrinth or working on a labyrinthian pattern for spellcraft. A watch tends to deter from that experience.

3. Quiet your mind. Try to release any expectations so the labyrinth's energy can reveal itself to you one step at a time. This is very important in planned and spontaneous activities. In these moments you may discover that the pattern you had in mind wasn't right at all or needs some minor alterations.

4. Bow slightly and reverently to the pattern. This acknowledges the sacred energies that already exist there, and those that are about to unfold before you.

5. If you wish, state a purpose. Something like "I am a seeker after truth" (or wisdom, knowledge, peace, health) is common for a declaration.

6. Trust your instincts and begin moving inward. (For people who are drawing, carving, or imagining a labyrinth, trace the pattern with your finger or visualize it instead.) As you go, cleanse and empty your mind of mundane thoughts (let go and let god/dess).

7. Participate wholly in the experience, don't just observe others or your environment. Think about each sense and what it's experiencing.

8. Take labyrinth walking at your own pace, knowing that this rhythm may change throughout the activity depending on what's happening to you inwardly. Try taking regular deep breaths, in through your nose and out through your

mouth, so that your breathing's cadence follows your walking or working pace. This will help you set up a natural, comfortable tempo for the entire activity.

9. When anxiety arises, which is natural, work through it and try to discern its source. Many people report that this happens when walking, tracing, or drawing the turns and intersections (choice-making areas).

10. Stay in the moment. Remain open and allow. Don't push aside any flashes of creativity or insight that come to you as you might normally. The labyrinth has a tendency to set these off, no matter what your purpose in walking it may have been.

11. If at any time you find that you've lost your way in the labyrinth, stop. Consider if you simply got distracted or if this momentary disorientation is a message. Ask yourself: Have you lost your way spiritually, physically, mentally, or emotionally, especially with regard to the present goal? When you answer that question, you can then get your bearings and either continue or start over to repattern a more positive outcome.

12. You will reach the center when you *know* you are there. Here you meet both sounds and silences, trust and doubt, your past and future, the temporal and eternal. Embrace all; acknowledge all. It can be a very emotional moment. Let-tears, singing, or other expressions happen of their own accord.

It's interesting to note that historians believe there was once the image of a minotaur in the center of the Knossos labyrinth. This represents our inner shadows; the monsters we must overcome (like apathy, fear, and jealousy) before we can leave the "point" of the rosette and return to the world with magick in our back pocket.

How you overcome your monster is up to you. Some kill it; others make peace with it. Both options have symbolic value to consider in your activities.

13. Stay in the center of the labyrinth, working with that energy, until your burdens fall aside and give way to joy, presence, and being. This is the labyrinth's gift to experience and integrate on your way back out into the "real" world. At this point you will no longer struggle to "fit into" anyone else's expectations, but instead find a way of living that fits who you are.

14. Begin walking the outward bound path or applying the pattern you've created. Some people report the overwhelming desire to skip, dance, twirl, or other expressive movements that depict what they've discovered. This type of action also "spins" the magick the labyrinth created!

15. Bow again to the labyrinth upon completing your activity, in effect thanking it for whatever you've gained from the experience. This also honors, again, the sacred presences invoked by the pattern.

At this juncture I also suggest writing down everything you can recall from the whole activity in a personal or magickal diary. If it helps, note the specifics of what you felt and sensed, point by point, at each of the previous fourteen steps. This writing frees our natural ability to help us integrate knowledge. These notes house many of the labyrinths' lessons to you—ones that you will want to return to and meditate upon.

The labyrinth's pattern does not stop influencing your life when the "walk" is over. The pattern continues to resonate in your aura for a long time, slowly untangling itself and shifting energies. Consequently, it's not uncommon for people to experience difficulty in verbalizing or explaining their labyrinthian experiences to others for days, months, and even years. The labyrinth's imprint works slowly on human perception, leaving its ghostly shape and its unique motion laid out in our mind. This acts like a subtle blueprint for contacting and expressing the Sacred, which is something only you can qualify and quantify for yourself. If you can't express that to others, don't worry about it. The process of getting there and the inward reality that results is far more important.

Planned or Spontaneous?

Your labyrinth-walking activities can be planned or spontaneous. In planned labyrinths, make sure your path's pattern, edge, and number of turns correspond with the goal (like using a four-course, hand-drawn design in shades of green and gold as a charm to improve financial stability). In spontaneous activities, where you simply draw a pattern while thinking about the issue at hand, use the traditional labyrinth symbolism for interpretive values *first*, followed by reviewing Part 2 for more insight to any manifested pattern with whose symbolism you may be unfamiliar.

Sample Labyrinth Activities

This chapter has provided you with some labyrinth-walking exercises to try already. Even so, there are many more ways that you can apply the labyrinth's energy patterns to your life and needs. Here are just a few more illustrations to consider, try, and/or adapt:

The Birthday Labyrinth

On your birthday when you have a few moments alone, copy a labyrinth from this book. Color the path going into the center with hues that represent your past. If you wish, draw little emblems that symbolize important junctures in that past along the inbound path (note that these should be historically progressive—the oldest event being first and the more recent closer to the center).

When you reach the center, light a small candle there (you can affix this to the paper if you want, or just have a candle near your activity on which to focus your attention). Leave behind the things from the past you no longer need or want. Rejoice in the person you are today and in your blessings. Blow out the candle and make a wish for the future.

Now, start looking at the outbound path. For what do you hope? Of what do you dream in your future? Color this part of the labyrinth with hues and symbols that represent those hopes and dreams. Keep this token with you for the whole year (perhaps folded carefully into a wallet). When you come to the next birthday labyrinth exercise, look at the future path from this first activity and see what wishes the pattern helped you manifest over the last year!

Commitment or Marriage Labyrinth

A love knot has nothing on the labyrinth for building energies that support a strong and healthy relationship. Within this safe confine, marriage can begin positively because both people come to the center willingly—they come as themselves in total truthfulness. Here nothing hides from the Sacred or each other. Consequently, I can think of no better pattern in which to make an engagement proposal, a commitment to live together, or a declaration of one's vows.

In either case, this particular labyrinth needs to be BIG. You will both want to be able to stand in the middle comfortably and walk the labyrinth pattern together. Around the path, I would suggest leaving symbolic tokens that represent what you have built in your relationship up to this point, and what you hope for in the future. Exchanging gifts at the center is perfectly apt, as is having a celebration or jumping a broomstick as you exit the pattern. In this case what awaits you on the other side of the labyrinth is nothing less than a new life where two become as one!

Chakra Labyrinth

Make a seven-circuit labyrinth on a large piece of cloth (big enough that you can walk the pattern). Paint each of the circuits a different color of the rainbow, beginning with red on the outer edge (akin to a traditional mandala) followed by yellow, green, blue, indigo, and ending in violet at the center. Each one of these will represent your chakras from the base to the crown [root, sacral, solar plexus, heart, throat, third eye, and crown].

Bow to the labyrinth before starting, acknowledging it as part of yourself. As you walk the first color, focus on physical matters and the element of earth. As you walk yellow, direct your attention to the water element and the balance of emotions versus intellect. You should start to feel energy rising from your feet up to your solar plexus at this point.

Continue forward, meditating on the heart of your spiritual life throughout the green circuit. When you enter blue, consider the power in your name and the potential in words as a sacred force for manifesting magick. When the labyrinth turns indigo it signals another shift in your awareness from the lower to higher self—to the domain of visions and dreams. Stay open to insights from outside yourself, inspired by the divine.

Finally on the seventh circuit you reach a point of decision-making or thankfulness, and sometimes both. Whatever things came to light on the first six turns will culminate on this last circuit so you can integrate the experience on your way back out. Notice too that by now your whole body is vibrating with energy. Your forehead might even tingle or feel light from it all. This is quite natural. Let it happen and move very slowly so as to not disrupt the magick. Make notes of your experience while still in a heightened state of awareness, then ground out by eating some raw vegetables.

By the way, those of you who would like to try this but don't have the space available for a large effort, you can make a painting of this labyrinth pattern and meditate on it instead. Visualize each color on the path as pouring up from the ground and through the chakra points for the first three points. Continue with one color until that area hums with energy, then move on to the next. Visualize colored light coming down from above for the last four.

Group Work

During the Renaissance historians documented one family by the name of Gonzaga. This family had a labyrinth painted on a wooden ceiling that was used for group meditations. This might seem odd if you don't see the labyrinth's pattern as a unifying symbol and its power as a spiritual tool. This family obviously appreciated both, and in so doing they left us with a thought to ponder—that being the question of working with families in the labyrinth motif.

When we look at our family units against the backdrop of modern responsibilities, there seems to be little opportunity for strengthening that unit. The Gonzagas may have given us a clue however—that of gathering together to meditate on the labyrinth and gather unity from the experience. This approach allows you to consider each individual as they interact with the whole when constructing the activity. It also allows the leader to take into account the pace set by the whole. The ultimate goal here is to reach the destination together, using focus and a keen awareness of one another's energy as a guide.

An alternative to meditating on the labyrinth that's more suited to small children with short attention spans is that of walking a labyrinth. Again, a leader with a good feeling for the entire group can make this experience one that everyone partakes of together, one step at a time. In either case, it's recommended that the individuals partaking of the activity do rhythmic matched breathing exercises beforehand to try to bring their auras into harmony with each other.

After everyone is in sync, consider tying a ribbon around the first participant's waist, leaving five feet of ribbon between each person, and so on down the line. The second person begins walking the labyrinth when the ribbon shows signs of tautness. This accomplishes several things. First, no one gets left behind or feels like a wallflower. Second, the tether forces everyone to be more sensitive to each other's pace. Third, symbolically the ribbon ties everyone together—a strong symbol of unity that still offers independence.

When you reach the center of your activity, that's the time for a group hug. If you want to discuss anything in an open, honest fashion, now's the time to do so. Then remove the tether and let each individual move out from the center at their own pace. Again, this stresses that while a family is a "unit" each person in that unit has value in, and of, themselves. Discuss the experience afterward over your favorite family foods.

Liberation, Hastening, Safety, and Abundance Labyrinth

There is an old custom in India where people place saffron water on the belly of a pregnant woman and draw a labyrinth. The woman then drinks some of this blessed water to hasten childbirth. This is a marvelous example of the labyrinth weaving its path into folk customs. Another good example comes from Scandinavian sailors. When they wanted an abundant catch or good weather, they would walk the labyrinth before setting sail, or build one on the shore.

Adapting these ideas a bit, make a saffron tincture (a potion created by steeping a few sprigs in warm water). For liberation this might be most effective if prepared during a new or waning moon. For hastening or abundance, a waxing or full moon is better.

When your tincture is prepared, with the pointer finger of your strong hand draw a labyrinth pattern in the water. Keep your mind keenly on the area of your life you want liberated, where you need abundance, something you need to manifest quickly. This can apply to creativity (overcoming blockage), increasing cash flow, or aiding the results of spellcraft, just to name a few. When you complete the pattern, drink the water. The act of drawing the pattern in water evokes the energy, then drinking the water symbolically accepts the freedom represented.

Prayer Labyrinth

Several chapels house labyrinth images outside the sanctum. Before the seeker enters, they trace the image with a finger while reciting a prayer. What this person may not know, however, is that tracing the pattern itself is a kind of prayer—to become one again with the Source, and to know the self. It's an important prayer and one you can recreate with ease at any time, anywhere you wish.

Simply carry a labyrinth pattern with you. When you need spiritual focus, support, or guidance, trace the pattern with your pointer finger. If you wish, recite a prayer inwardly or out loud while your finger guides you through the twists and turns of the labyrinth, into the center and back out. Take your time, moving slowly and deliberately. By the time you reach the other side, you should feel some of the stress waning, and a sense of hope filling your heart. Repeat as desired!

Mirror Labyrinth

An exhibit in 1981 included da Vinci's mirror closet as the center of a labyrinth. This closet had eight sides, all mirrored, to symbolize the meeting of, and perfecting of, self. From this room a person could emerge in full awareness, being reborn.

Adapting this idea a bit, try making this charm for personal awareness and wholeness. Begin by copying or making a labyrinth pattern that really appeals to your higher senses. When the drawing is complete, put a small mirror (or mirrored surface) in the very center. Whenever you feel unsure of your way, look to the mirror and trust yourself! Carry this often.

Post-Labyrinth Mandala

This is a really neat way to bring two sacred patterns together. After you've completed any type of labyrinth activity, follow it up with a mandala design. Go to the next chapter and review the steps to creating a spontaneous mandala, then make one that expresses whatever you felt you accomplished with the exercise you just undertook. This picture will be well worth the little extra time it takes to make, as it will portray visually what's happening inwardly. In this form it can become a charm or amulet that inspires ongoing transformation!

Some people who go through a labyrinth say they feel driven as if by some inexplicable force. This drive fascinates, liberates, and also seems oddly familiar even to those who have never walked the path before. As the seeker continues, this drive develops and shifts, unfolding emotions, memories, and many other dynamics of the great human experience. Effectively, the labyrinth becomes midwife for our awakening—awakening to all facets and potentials of being human—awakening to what this truly means not only in daily life but in our never-ending spiritual quest. Stay awake!

Diagram of the Guhyasamaja Mandala

3

MANDALAS: YOUR SPIRITUAL STRATEGY

Orient yourself toward this one point and nothing will be impossible to you.

—Buddha

A galaxy is a mandala in space. The earth is a mandala, Stonehenge is a mandala, a bird's nest is a mandala, and a bonsai tree is a mandala. It seems no matter where you look—from a cell's design to the unfolding stars at night—the mandala's sacred pattern is everywhere, and that's exactly what makes mandalas so special.

The word mandala is sometimes translated as meaning a sphere of essence. In regions where this symbol is used frequently it represents inner harmony, an awareness of our personal power, the ability to extend compassion selflessly, the growth of wisdom, and the ultimate wholeness of enlightenment. By its very nature a mandala mirrors all life, all diversity, and portrays the soul's heritage as an eternal citizen. All this contained neatly within a circle, centered around a specific point.

Speaking of points, how often have you heard the phrase "missing the point"? This is a key to understanding the mandala and its magickal function. Historically speaking, mandala-styled art appeared and reappeared during times of chaos. For example, during the Crusades gothic motifs depict amazing mandalas in stained glass and wood as if to repattern the world when humans as a whole were missing the point. In a similar manner, each mandala you undertake poses this question: Are you missing the point spiritually? If so, the mandala stands ready to guide you back to that monad.

Remember when you were a kid and spun around in circles? If you kept your eyes on one point, in a technique called spotting, you never got dizzy or lost your way. You also unknowingly made yourself into a mandala in motion. Now, let's take this idea one step further.

The goal of labyrinth walking is to spin the magick without losing our focus, and open ourselves to new possibilities. To accomplish this we need to keep our eyes on the right spot! This spot is the center point of the mandala which, as we move toward it, turns out to be the core of our being as it mingles with the Sacred. In that magickal moment, a person can begin to see that knowledge and intuition can work cooperatively, and that each person is a co-creator with the god/dess.

In reading about mandalas in this chapter and considering your own mandala creations in various media, keep this central point in mind. Also stop to consider for a moment that the labyrinth also has a point that connects with Sacred energies. This means that (if you wish) labyrinth symbolism can intertwine with that of the mandala into a kind of waltz where the mundane and spiritual balance, interact, and finally manifest in your goal.

Reinventing the Wheel

Mandala also means a circle—both its circumference and its center point—but mandalas haven't always been circular. Some are square, triangular, polygonal, and even almond shaped (more correctly called a Mandorla). In magickal traditions, however, the circular mandala has certainly been the most popular.

One example of this magickal motif is easily seen in the Wheel of Destiny (or Wheel of Fortune) depicted in many Tarot decks. When this card appears in a reading, it represents the active hand of fate because the wheel is always in motion. It reminds us that we must descend to rise, dream to realize, think to act, close to open, give to receive, and live to BE.

Wheel of Destiny Reflection

This card of the Tarot is a good one to ponder in an effort to better understand the significance of circles, cycles, and the magickal significance of mandalas:

Take three deep cleansing breaths, then look at the details on this card. Consider how each aspect of the wheel (color, placement, surroundings, etc.) represents your life, which is ever turning, and ever changing. You have traveled far to reach this point, and learned much. Yet as this mandala moves along its path, it beckons to you—whispering of your ongoing spiritual quest, and of the road that still lies ahead. The wheel's motion never ceases, pressing you onward. It will be up to you to decide what to do with that road and how to handle its challenges.

It is no coincidence that the wheel's number is ten. One is the line, zero the point of the mandala, and with these two numbers an entire binary language is born. It is the ancient language of karma, fate, and destiny as written in the matrix of your soul.

Listen to the words of this language. They're familiar and haunting. Feel the energy in the air; visualize the power as the mandala speaks to you through its motion. Remember: when we stop moving and changing we die inside. So be aware of your motion, of your aliveness, of being!

Did you notice too that the person in this illustration holds the Destiny Wheel in hand, and is in fact pushing it? This represents control—your ability to be a co-creator and make the most of your life and magick. It can begin today. Become the mandala!

The second example is that of the magick circle, drawn around the center point of the altar, danced around the altar, linked hand to hand around the altar with the elements. In ancient times the circle was physically sketched on the floor or in the dirt to pattern the power around the magus for safety. Modern practitioners still set up symbolic points (mini-altars) for the circle, asperge the circle's circumference with water, or visualize the line between the worlds as filled with light. This line, be it physical or astral, is just as important to the mandala as is the point—it represents the boundaries we give ourselves in life and in magick.

Creating a Magick Circle Mandala

For this activity you'll need the following: an old sheet; yellow, blue, red, black, and green fabric paint; a pencil; a paint brush; and a ruler. Optional tools include some new age music and sandalwood incense to create a positive magickal atmosphere.

Cut out a square from the old sheet, one large enough to use in your rituals given the amount of floor space available. Iron it so it's flat. In the middle of this square write your magickal name with the black paint. This is the point of your mandala. It is from this point that you will spin the magick out to bless yourself, others, or the world.

Using your ruler, make eight equal-length lines extending out from the point using a pencil. This will look like an eight-pointed star and represents radiating magickal energy. Once you're happy with the way these are placed, paint them in black too.

Look at the wheel before you. It has four distinct quarters (one at each of the four cardinal directions). Paint each one of those quarters with its elemental color (red—south; blue—west; green—north; yellow—east). As you paint each quarter, focus on the energy represented by the color, direction, and element. If you wish, you can invoke that Power or perhaps chant something suited to the element to further energize the mandala. Here's one example of a simple invocation that can be spoken at the respective points of the wheel as indicated:

East: *By breath and wind, let this magick begin!*
South: *With warmth and fire, build the energy higher!*
West: *Through water and waves, the pattern is saved!*
North: *From soil and earth, this mandala is birthed!*

Next, put the black border on your magick circle if you wish, but leaving the line off might be more appropriate (to represent limitlessness). Some people also like to blend all four colors together over their magickal name to represent the meeting place between the worlds, and the right balance of energies so magick flows most effectively.

Let this dry completely and follow the directions given on the fabric paint to make sure the colors set properly. You can now put this on the floor at any time (anywhere) as a portable mandala and sacred space where you are the point!

Magickal practitioners certainly aren't the only ones to have put the symbolism of the circular mandala to good use. If we look at

the mandala's history, its easy to see that this pattern has fasci-
nated humankind for a very long time.

The Mandala's Legacy

The mandala's legacy is quite extensive, and reviewing it reveals
a prevailing theme. The Aborigines in Australia, monks in Tibet,
tribal communities in Mexico, and the peoples of Mesopotamia
and Nepal, all used mandalas of concentric circles to represent the
universe's fundamental force and the progression of the human
soul. It was a cosmic egg mandala, for example, that gave birth to
the universe. The sun's sphere is a mandala that humankind
trusted in designing calendar patterns. But it doesn't end there.

Mandala Divination

This is fun to do for friends on New Year's Day or a birthday.
Have them sit down and draw a twelve-segment circle with
one item or symbol in each slice of the circle while thinking
about the upcoming year. You could have tokens on hand for
them to place in the circle instead, but I personally recommend the drawing process so querent can carry the finished
mandala as a charm afterwards.

The symbol placed in the first segment to the right of "noon"
represents what to expect in the present month. The item
placed in the second segment clockwise represents the coming
month. This progression continues clockwise around the circle.

How do you interpret the pictures? You can use a dream
dictionary or any good book on divination like *Futuretelling*
(Crossing Press, 1998). Or better still, trust your instincts! For
example, someone who sketched a pen in month six might
need to focus on their communication skills that month.
Alternatively this object might portend an important letter or
bit of news arriving. Get creative!

Many Native Americans used medicine wheels and shields to symbolize the universe, transformation, life's cycles, and our growth as people. While they do not call these wheels "mandalas" the parallels are uncanny, and the symbols are still in use. Additionally, the ancient shamans often used circles for casting-styled divination. After the cast, they did not read any object that landed outside that circle because this boundary represented the querent's life and/or question. The pattern within the circle was interpreted, with the center often indicating intimate information about the querent, or present circumstances. It was the "point."

Meanwhile across the ocean Celtic people ate in circles to emphasize unity. By so doing they became a mandala of individuals whose point is the whole. Hermetics, Alchemists, and Kabbalists all used geometric designs, often within a circle, as a way of trying to unlock mystical and natural mysteries. The Whirling Dervishes danced a mandala pattern to participate in oneness with the Sacred and manifest that harmony. They danced to become the point in body, mind, and spirit.

Mandalas appeared in Christian tradition too. St. Hildegard received visions of visually stunning mandalas and then used them in her teachings and healing methods. Jakob Boehme, a Christian mystic, represented his beliefs in the mandala form by illustrating spirit and matter as intimately intertwined in his writings. Certain pieces of medieval Christian art and architecture show a circular universe superimposed over a cross (a symbol of the four corners of creation) with angels who keep time's wheel marching forward, empowered by God. Similarly, Judaic mystics (Kabbalists) portrayed the universe moving around a wheel with God outside the mandala as if watching over it.

In Nepal, India, and other parts of the world, the body's energy centers have also long been represented as swirling mandala-like circles. Commonly called chakras, an adept practitioner can activate these energy centers progressively during meditation, beginning at the base of the back and ending at the crown of the head. This last center, or doorway, creates an opening through which the Sacred can communicate, and magickal energy flows.

Chakra Meditation

To try this meditation you should give yourself about twenty minutes alone where you won't be disturbed.

Sit or lie comfortably, but in a position where you won't fall asleep. Visualize your body as it is right now. Focus your attention progressively on the points listed below. As you do, see each as a tight dot of swirling light moving clockwise if you wish to open the dot, or counterclockwise if you need to close it a little. For example, if you need to tone down empathic tendencies, you might want to close your heart chakra and third eye chakra a bit during times when you're around a lot of people.

If you're opening a chakra, visualize it growing slowly and steadily larger over the area noted. If you're closing it, see it shrinking until you feel the difference is sufficient for the situation at hand. And, if trying to awaken all of them, begin at the root chakra and work up *slowly*. Sit for a while experiencing this openness, making mental notes of the experience, then adjust each chakra so it's comfortable for daily life before returning to normal awareness.

By the way, you can learn a lot about yourself and your present condition by paying attention to the way your chakras appear astrally at the outset of this meditation. For example, if a person sees his or her throat chakra as very tiny or missing, it indicates a tendency to bite one's tongue rather than speaking out on important issues. Or, seeing a huge heart chakra might indicate a tendency toward letting one's emotions control things, or for being overly romantic.

Root Chakra: (base of spine near genitals): Often seen as red in color, this chakra controls human basics like the flight or flee instinct and sexuality.

Navel Chakra: Often seen as dark blue in color, this chakra controls our sense of balance both physically and spiritually. It also represents our connection with all things, as a symbol of the center of the universe.

Solar Plexus Chakra: Often seen as yellow in color, this represents both our ambitions and fears.

Heart Chakra: Often seen as green, this is our emotional center, self awareness, and our ability to love.

Throat Chakra: Often seen as blue, this represents the power of the word and our communications.

Third Eye Chakra: The psychic center; the active visionary aspect of humankind and our sense of orientation to the greater scheme of things.

Crown Chakra: Seen as purple (denoting divine connections), this represents our ability to remain open to Spirit and spiritual matters. It also connects with higher thinking.

Yogis have gotten a little more creative with this whole idea, making their bodies into living mandalas for worship, meditation, and prayer. They believe that specific body positions help make them one with the pattern, and therefore with the magick of that pattern. The goal here is to awaken and liberate the spirit to the elements, to the design, and to the One by working with the patterns of, and then moving past, physicality.

In many of these settings the act of drawing the mandala or focusing on it was believed to evoke the ongoing motion of the cosmos, and everything within that vastness including the human spirit. Yet in an odd dichotomy, Hindu and Buddhist tradition reveals that the goal of the mandala was not always to be in motion. Instead the hope was to rediscover stillness—to reunite with the center of the mandala (the Sacred), and find the quiet of the soul.

To accomplish this the Buddhist ritually creates an imaginary palace during meditation. In enlightened form a person is no longer physical, so this mind's-eye mandala becomes a body for the meditator—a celestial body with tremendous significance. Each part of the greater whole represents a guiding principle for that person, and each mandala offers a different lesson.

Harmonious Home Mandala

Since one of the goals of mandala making is to promote still-ness and peace, it's an activity very suited to family environments. For this activity, divide a circle into equal parts, one for each member of your household. Have each person color or draw in one space while focusing on thoughts of unity, accord, love, and cooperation. When the mandala is done, protect it with art spray and hang it near your doorway as a gentle reminder of the sacredness of home and family. Some people like to touch the center of this mandala upon leaving or entering the home to symbolically keep the family moving toward the point—toward wholeness.

Note: if you live alone, this is a good activity for privacy or banishing negativity.

Moving closer to the present day, Carl Jung felt the center of the mandala represented the total human personality, and that the edge designated the safe haven within which each of us keeps ourself (our personal space and chosen environments).

He said that these images as a whole symbolize our ability to "fill out" the patterns of our lives, and even exceed them. To quote from his work *Mandala Symbolism* (p. v):

> Only gradually did I discover what the mandala really is—Formation, Transformation, Eternal Mind's eternal creation. And that is the self, the wholeness of the personality which if all goes well is harmonious, but which cannot tolerate self deceptions. In this respect, the mandala that any individual creates is a highly personal process. There can be no "right" or "wrong" about it, only be-ing, experiencing, and understanding the path to the center.

Note that the path to the center here has strong labyrinth overtones!

Today we still find the mandala interacting with humankind on an intimate level, attempting to pattern order out of disorder, and unity out of discord. Some holisticians, for example, use the patterns to augment physical and emotional healing. Similarly, the Navajos use the center of a mandala-styled sand painting to promote wholeness, and Buddhist monks continue to use the mandala as a tool for realizing spiritual principles and augmenting meditative practices.

With all this in mind, the mandala's pattern can be magickally applied as a tool for:

- Comprehending and appreciating the functions of diversity. Here the mandala expresses variety, which is both the point of the mandala and its boundaries (and even beyond).

- Healing rituals and spells. The exterior of the mandala (its boundary) creates a womb in which we can renew and restore ourselves.

- Recognizing spiritual principles (and integrating them). Here, the point of the mandala is the principle, while everything around it expresses that idea in symbolic form.

- Bringing order to chaos. This type of mandala might have a very loose exterior, but a far more concrete point—the goal toward which you're working.

- Establishing tranquility over trauma. A well-ordered, well-balanced mandala encourages similar symmetry.

- Improving your ability to focus and center (again moving toward "the point").

- Cultivating meditative skills. Creating mandalas is, in itself, a meditative experience because you translate thought into symbols and imagery (even as you might in visualization).

- Unlocking soul memory. A mandala in which the point is recognizing past lives can manifest symbols of those lives when the creator is in the right spiritual state of mind.

- Discerning fate's hand at work. The patterns that sometimes appear outside the boundaries of the mandala indicate outside forces, including destiny.

- Rediscovering inner peace and happiness by accepting your role as a co-pilot in life with the Sacred. While mandalas can have other points besides this, ultimately the highest goal is reuniting with the monad.

- Motivating progress, breaking old cycles, or creating new cycles. The mandala is in motion, so when you put symbols of progress into that whole, it motivates progress. Simlarly, destroying a mandala that represents the "old ways" and creating a new one helps recreate the pattern in a positive way.

- Stressing unity and harmony: The circle of our life is nothing without the point and the point nothing without the circle. Knowing this helps a person return to balance and a place of acceptance.

- Finding a magickal path that's wholly right for you: If you draw a mandala of a path you're considering, it will show you many questions, reservations, or confirmations about that choice that you may not be able to access consciously.

- Spinning and directing energy: Since the mandala is in motion, moving with that ongoing motion will help us better direct our energy on all levels of being, including magickally.

From this brief review we can see that the mandala holds great potential for anyone on a metaphysical path. Its patterns help us form a good strategy for manifesting our magick and our spiritual nature. The mandala also challenges us to leave behind our shadows and follow the path of "light" so we can become fulfilled, empowered, and whole.

The Modern Rebirth: Tibetan Sand Mandalas

The beautiful sand mandalas created by Tibetan monks are among the best known spiritual artforms with a long-standing tradition. In Tibet, the word for mandala literally means "center of the universe in which a fully awakened being exists." I had the privilege of seeing one created at a local art gallery. As I watched, I realized that the mystical patterns of the mandala generate energy as they form (and sometimes upon disassembly). The very matrix of the design symbolizes perfection: perfected concentration for prayer and meditation, or the soul's perfection. As the mandala comes together, it manifests the pattern of healing, happiness, and life's continuance.

The process of making the mandala is very important to the whole creation (as was the labyrinth). This emphasis mirrors a central Buddhist philosophy that basically says the way one arrives at a point is just as important as the path taken or the point itself. Even this philosophy is patterned like a mandala (the circumference point tied together in place, time, and thought).

For those of you unfamiliar with the monk's techniques, they take a small tool filled with sand and run a rod along one jagged edge to create a vibration. Mystically this vibration becomes an element of the energy being created. Artistically, the gentle vibrations allow the creator to release minute amounts of sand at a time. This is pretty astounding to watch, but more amazing still is the fact that the sand mandalas are not flat. They have three dimensions through which the goal is communicated to the Universe—three levels to represent various levels of human understanding, and through which enlightenment can be achieved.

I tried to use the tool myself, but it takes a lot of practice and eye–hand coordination to get the technique to work. If you'd like to try something like this yourself, I recommend using dampened, colored sand instead (pretend you're building sand castles at the beach). The dampness here has symbolic value of bringing water to the barren wastelands (nourishing the spirit), and allows you to create your mandala in three dimensions with less difficulty.

You can often find colored sand at toy stores. If that's not available, buy some play sand and color it using food coloring. Put a cup of sand into a bowl with water and a few drops of the food coloring and stir. Leave the sand in this solution until it's saturated with the chosen hue. Drain off the extra water and let the sand dry a bit before using.

The key to success in building your sand mandala is remembering two words: *symmetry* and *point*. Mandalas always have some point around which they form, and have a sense of balance in their construction. Beyond that, the patterns are wholly up to you so long as they represent your goal. For example, if I created a mandala for healing, I might make a blue circle of sand, with a lighter blue circle within it, and then a white point (representing purity and completion). For me, blue is a very healing color and the circle symbolizes wholeness.

And what happens when you're done with this? Traditionally the sand is given to water or the winds so its magick can extend outward in all directions and heal the earth. If you're at a beach, just leave the creation where it is and let the tides greet and bear your energy. If not, try to find a living water source (one that's not stagnant) or wait for a gentle breeze to come along so you can sprinkle the sand into it. You might also want to keep a little of the multicolored sand to carry as an ongoing charm that attracts blessings and improves spiritual insight.

Traditional Mandala Symbolism

When you make mandalas it's nice to have some traditional symbolism to consider. The list that follows pertains specifically to the world's existing mandalas. While you certainly can use Part 2 of this book to assist in designing magickal mandalas, these particular emblems may prove even more powerful and thought provoking.

The repeated appearance of certain designs in mandalas, all of which have interrelated symbolic value, indicates something important, something to which we should pay attention. The duplication of a pattern, or very similar ones, makes a statement, a "point" for us to focus on. Think of this like a theme in a movie; the pattern is a mystical motif whose mysteries are waiting to be unraveled.

Additionally, it stands to reason that experts in mandala making would use the patterns known to be most effective in their efforts. I see no reason not to pragmatically follow their example, beginning with colors.

Color

Not all mandalas have color. In fact the best-known mandala, the yin–yang symbol, is simply black and white to represent polarity and balance. Even so, colors have been an important part of the human experience, often communicating ideas when words could not. Humans also have very strong psychological responses to color, so you may find yourself naturally drawn to specific ones for both planned and spontaneous mandala activities.

Here's a brief list of colors as they've been used in traditional mandalas. To this, by all means add your intuitive senses to know what color is best for any part of your mandala activity, or what the colors appearing in your spontaneous mandala exercises mean:

- black—our borders and personal boundaries; mysteries; obscurity (something hidden); formless potential that hasn't been awakened or realized; introspection; death (literal or figurative); the circumference

- blue—cool-headedness; feminine energies; fertility or abundance; truthfulness, honesty, and morality; vastness (like the sky); transcendence and overcoming; compassion and kindness; patience; sadness; the intuitive nature (sometimes a blue circle is depicted)

- gold—logos (the word, especially in sacred form like chanting or mantras); the god aspect; the sun or fire

- green—nature's gifts; hopefulness and expectation; faith and trust; nurturing growth; renewal or revitalization; jealousy (usually yellow-green)

- grey—neutrality; uncertainty; the wisdom of age

- orange—understanding that comes from experience; assertiveness; leadership; cooperation

- pink—tenderness; friendship; openness and accessibility; physicality (focus on the body and health)

- red—physical or emotional warmth; uplifting occasions; courage; passion; battles (the warrior's spirit coming forth); celebration of life; initiation; desire to thrive; transmutation of energies

- violet—holiness; dignity; mastery; the point

- white—purity and spirit; the creative spark; order; transformation and being prepared for change; wisdom; the
  goddess aspect; beyond the boundaries

- yellow—illumination and awakening; vision and clarity; communication; hope; spiritual wealth

If this proves too abbreviated, more information on colors as
they pertain to psychology and other sacred patterns can be
found in Part Two of this book.

Patterns

A review of historical mandalas can make a person dizzy. You
can never really tell if one moves inward or outward, where it
really begins or ends, just like eternity. The pattern is just as
enigmatic morally. Ethically, it is neither good nor bad; it is neu-
tral untapped potential. The way we apply the pattern is what
makes the difference. This leads me to believe that one of the
mandala's messages is that life, indeed, is what we make of it.

Even with all this mystery, however, the pattern of the mandala always has one or more messages just waiting for our discovery. Here are a few designs that were given interpretive value
or correspondences in various cultural settings, most predominantly in the region of India. You can use these to better understand your spontaneous mandalas, or in thematically constructing
purposeful ones (see *Walking the Mandala* later in this chapter):

- almond-shaped border—grace; living presently; adroitness;
  defying logic; miracles

- axis—stressing the point; x marks the spot; compartmen-
  talization

- bell—unlimited potential; openings

- border—the boundaries you put between yourself and others or the environment. The more distinct this is, the greater amount of privacy you desire
- buds—blossoming energy; spring; renewal; an opportunity that's just making itself known
- center—Buddha consciousness
- circle in a circle—the eye of god; external vision vs. internal understanding; the window of the soul
- clockwise swastika—the sun; acceptance (so be it)
- counterclockwise swastika—the moon; intuition; casting off the old ways
- cross (templar style)—revealing secrets; creating the astral temple for protection or worship (sacred space)
- diamond—clarity; the nature of the mind
- dots—the unknown; mysteries; an alternative point
- eggs—fertility; possibilities; emerging skills or talents
- ellipses—celestial movement and dynamics
- empty center—openness to change; a gap to fill; unrealized or untapped potential
- flames—summer; energy; the holy spirit; transformation
- gates—a waiting point between world and not-world, and leaving behind the temporal
- half circle—the element of water
- knots—alchemical transmutation; binding energy; restrictions; ties to people, places, or things
- leaves—change; fall-colored leaves indicate the harvest of one's labors
- lotus—purity, perfection, and enlightenment; a symbol also associated with teachers and masters

- rose—versatility; tolerance; promise keeping; universal thinking; the prophetic self
- ruptures in border—liberation; breaking away; intense emotion; extension of consciousness
- snowflake—individuality, winter (literal or figurative)
- square—earth; grounding and foundation; internalization
- thunderbolt—active compassion
- triangle (red)—the fire element
- wheel—perfecting one's character; cycles; time
- wheel (eight-spoked)—the Eightfold path of Buddhist beliefs that leads to perfection (the eight points being right belief, right resolution, right speech, right action, right living, right effort, right thinking, and peace of mind).

As with colors, many more potential patterns for your mandala activities can be found in Part Two of this book.

Segments and Points

One thing you'll notice about mandalas is that they frequently have a specific number of sections (akin to the turns of a labyrinth), cross-sections, or points, all of which have symbolic value as follows:

- No sections—these often occur in mandalas of self-expression or healing where the colors/shapes simply swirl but don't form any points or division. This occurs because while an individual is the sum of his or her experiences, those experiences mingle together to create the whole personality.

  This also happens with one-color mandalas. In this case the whole of the meaning lies in the color.

- One predominant point or section—this occurs when something in a person's life is being emphasized dramatically (for good or ill). Whatever that section represents needs to be scrutinized to determine whether the stress is necessary, or if something's being blown out of proportion.

- Two halves—polarity and balance; right brain/left brain; recognizing both god and goddess within; sometimes duality or division.

- Six segments—Star of David; protection; blessings. You can't lose with this pattern. It's good for just about any type of magick.

- Seven sections—harmony and hope. Highly recommended to offset the winter blues or chronic depression.

- Eight sections or points—rebirth; a new beginning. This pattern in a mandala will help to clear away old, outmoded thoughts or habits so you can begin fresh. It also represents devotion.

- Nine points—perfection; fruition; manifestation. An excellent motif to choose when you need something finalized or a sense of closure.

- Twenty-two points—manifesting god/dess' will. Note the clockwise progression of these points (and what they point to) to know what steps to take to make this happen.

- Twenty-four points—astrological influences. The colors or shapes at each point may reveal more. For example, if the point that corresponds with Pisces is black, it might indicate some type of creative blockage since Pisces often governs inventiveness or intuitiveness.

- Fifty-two points—the year or cycles. Pay particular attention to the order, color, and symbols at each point.

Note that the numeric correspondences provided here can also be applied to maze and labyrinth sections too.

Walking the Mandala

You now have enough information on hand to try making and walking the mandala in a way of your choosing. In considering this further, however, we have to look at two different types of mandala activities.

Spontaneous Mandalas

You will be using spontaneous mandalas to interpret various situations in your life, and what's happening in your inner world. For example, take a break right now and paint or draw a spontaneous mandala (try watercolors, colored inks, crayons, felt pens, or whatever suits your fancy). If it helps, start with a circle that has a point in the middle, then fill it in with doodles, geometrics, or other imagery that feels right. When you're done, look at what you've made and consider:

- Did you color in or outside the lines? The person who stays inside the lines prefers structure and order, and generally tries to remain within the confines provided by self, family, society, or culture. The person who goes outside the lines is a free thinker, dreamer, leader, or someone with a very strong presence. They are not afraid to extend the mandala beyond what we can see and touch.

- Do you like what you see? A person who doesn't is either going through a difficult time, or lacks self-esteem.

- Are you being honest? When you answered the second question, were you truthful with yourself? When you created the mandala, did you try to contrive it in a particular fashion or just let yourself go? This is very important. For spontaneous efforts to be helpful you have to liberate yourself, be truthful, and be real.

- Now look at the pattern. Does it have a motif of color or form? If so, what immediate impression does it make?

If it doesn't seem to have any particular meaning at first glance, break it down into individual forms and look those up in Part 2. For example, a flower mandala that has six dew-laden petals is displaying three different elements—the flower, the number six, and the dewdrops (which might be found under tear or water). I would interpret this mandala very positively. Six indicates an overcoming of difficulty, often personal failure. As a result, the flower of your spirit is opened to the light and is being nourished (the dewdrop).

Taking this activity one step further, make a spontaneous mandala each morning for a week. At the end of the week take the following steps:

1. Review the mandalas in sequence and as a whole. Think of this like a book without words. What is it telling you?
2. Give each mandala a title, then title the whole week. (Don't think too much about this. Use one or two words that come immediately to mind.)
3. Label each form within the mandala. (If you don't want to write on the finished picture, make a list of key words underneath.)
4. Examine the mandalas by the previously given guidelines, then consider the symbolic language further by asking yourself:

   • What was this week's central theme? If for example, there was a lot of jagged red configurations in many of the mandalas, the theme may have been anger or stress (which likely means you need a break).

   • How do these images reflect your daily self dynamics? For example, do the images seem to flow from one to another or are they very choppy? This will tell you how much of one day, or one experience, carried over into the next.

   • What do the colors reveal of your energy levels? Very dark colors often indicate lagging or depressed physical, emotional, or spiritual energy. Over time this can lead to depression or illness, so try to root out the source by examining other aspects of the mandala. For example, if the dark color hovers over a symbol or itself is made into a shape, that symbol/shape is very likely the key to turning this situation around.

• Did you create anything wholly unexpected? A lot of people report that they created a mandala that seemed in total opposition to thoughts at that moment. Don't let this jar you. The mandala works intuitively and subtly, tapping into and effecting your unconscious mind, so the "feeling" and result isn't always concrete. Here form and meaning work together, often without any words to adequately express the outcome of that partnership.

You can make spontaneous mandalas any time you feel so inspired: a lunch break at work, a quiet moment late at night, your birthday, or whenever, and then interpret them using your own insights, the correspondences in this chapter, and Part 2 of this book. If you're feeling out of sorts, however, I recommend interpreting the mandala later when your mood is better, otherwise your results will be disappointing.

Say, for example, that someone's upset about a job. He or she draws a mandala hoping to better understand the underlying energies at work and interprets it immediately, while still distressed. This individual is likely to see the worst-case scenario (like being fired) because negative emotions were clouding his or her perspective, leading to the wrong conclusion about what the mandala represents.

So, while you want to examine your spontaneous mandalas in a timely manner, be wise about it. Know yourself well enough to recognize when it's best to wait.

Planned Mandalas

Planned mandalas are patterns that you research and create for specific purposes in much the same way as the labyrinth.

These patterns are laid out so they suit the application you have in mind (charms, rituals, and the other examples given in Chapter 1). There are two unique factors to consider in planned mandala-walking activities, though, that set them apart from mazes and labyrinths.

First, the mandala visually moves both outward and inward. You can certainly begin making or using it at either point. Start from the center when you want to unfold energy or the power of a pattern. Start at the outer edge when you want to integrate the pattern. But, because of the mandala's "get to the point" emphasis, it is often more traditional to move toward the center slowly. The symbolism equates to moving away from the exterior world to embrace inner knowingness.

The ancient mandala makers believed that every time a person undertakes a new pattern and follows it through to the point, he or she will recognize a new truth. Each new truth leads the participant back to the point yet again. While this all sounds very circular, it's meant to. Remember that the circumference and the point are one in mandala ideology.

Second, mandala-walking activities often include the recital of mantras, the most common being *om* or *om ah hum,* each syllable of the latter corresponding to the crown, throat, and heart chakra respectively. Repeating these sounds and letting them vibrate through our bodies (and the room) helps make a person one with all that has been and all that will be; it creates a harmony with the evolving pattern both within and without. It helps us successfully reach the point.

Now, that's not to say that labyrinth and maze activities can't employ this technique. It's just that mantras are distinctively suited to mandala walking, and it has been part of their design process for thousands of years. This makes mantras a tradition well worth considering in our mandala-related activities. One in particular that's comfortable on Western tongues is simply saying "I am." These two words represent and reaffirm presence, aliveness, and individuality (it is both part of the point and the whole, like the mandala itself).

Sample Mandala Activities

This chapter has already provided several mandala activities. For time-challenged readers like myself, or those who have difficulty finding creative ways to apply the mandala pattern to various situations, several more follow here.

Please don't just dive blindly into these activities. Read them over. Alter them so they have more meaningful symbols. Add sensual dimensions to them. Taking just a few moments to make these personal changes will make your mandala-walking activities far more successful, not only for these illustrations but for any you undertake.

Physical Mandala

For this activity, lie on the floor with your arms and legs extended so you form a star. Your head is the top of the star, your arms and legs form the other four points like a pentagram. By so doing, you are becoming a mandala in which your heart chakra is the "point" and the invisible circle of your aura is the circumference.

When you're stretched out and relaxed, close your eyes and begin to visualize a light in the center of your being (somewhere near your heart). This light represents your spirit. This is the foundation from where you build your relationship with the Sacred.

Now, let that light begin to grow brighter and spread out in the pattern of the star that you have made from your body. The metaphysical energy will naturally follow the pathways, the patterns you've provided for it physically! Proceed very slowly, as if saturating each cell touched by the light with spiritual power.

Go one step further and let the energy overflow into your auric envelope. The image this produces often looks like your body is glowing in the center of a swirling bubble of colored fireflies extending a foot or so beyond your skin. Take some time now to notice how this feels—how connected you are to self

and spirit at this moment—how smooth your aura is and how
that naturally puts you at ease. At this very moment you have
achieved the mandala. You are both the point and whole, and it
is adding to your well-being.

When you're ready, return to normal awareness. Make notes
of the experience in your journal. You can repeat this activity
any time you feel detached or withdrawn, to bolster personal
energy, or to augment health.

By the way, readers who enjoy yoga, or who are interested in
studying it, can use this activity as part of the various physical
postures of this art. The exercise will improve your spiritual
understanding of the bodily pattern, help in adjusting chakras,
and also assist with integrating and expressing the healthy energies that yoga produces.

A Burning Mandala

Some mandalas have been used to invite sacred energies into
an initiation ceremony, often by burning the mandala as an
offering. This activity is a slight adaptation of that idea. Begin by
making a goal-oriented mandala or perhaps copy on a plain
white piece of paper one from this chapter that inspires you.
Pierce the point of your chosen mandala with a stick of incense
so the mandala sits around the middle point of the incense (a
point within a point). Put one end of the incense into a fire-safe
container with a large base around it filled with sand or dirt (the
base should be the same diameter or larger than the mandala for
safety reasons).

Light the incense and begin to chant or incant something
suited to the theme of the mandala you've chosen. Say, for
example, you've made a tranquility mandala. In this case you
might say something like *peace, peace, peace . . . never cease, never
cease* all the while the incense burns. If you wish, change your
incantation so it honors a divine persona, or pick the scent of

your incense according to that goal (in this example lavender or something similar).

Let the incense burn down, catching the mandala on fire. Watch and focus as the mandala disappears completely, releasing its energy. Although the symbol is gone, its pattern remains in the air and in your life.

By the way, since this activity includes the element of fire, you might want to choose a mandala pattern suited to fiery energy. One example for energy that creates a positive change in your life would be eight flame-shaped petals coming out from the center point where you put the incense.

If you wish, retain the ashes from this activity and blend them with sand for making pre-energized sand mandalas!

Molded Mandalas

An alternative to the sand mandalas discussed earlier this chapter is clay (or perhaps salt dough for children). Both can create a three-dimensional finished look, speaking to all levels of human awareness (body-mind-spirit). Mind you, if you prefer to carve wood or chisel stone, those are perfectly good options too.

For clay, consider using a brand that's pre-colored, or a self-hardening clay that you can paint later to add color symbolism. For wood or stone, work in a base medium that makes sense in terms of your goal. For example, oak wood is a great option for a mandala designed to help reinforce your foundations (your point). For stone, I recommend soapstone. It's soft, carves easily with a minimum amount of tools (files, picks, and/or carving knives), and has a great textural appeal (it's very satiny).

For another sensual dimension, clay takes very well to having a drop or two of aromatic oil added to it. You can also rub oil into your wood. Soapstone is porous so a dab or two of oil won't hurt it, and the powder generated by carving is perfectly suited to wearing as body talc! In this case you can literally "put on" the pattern of what you've designed in the stone medium.

Choose your oil so that it corresponds with the goal indicated by the mandala pattern, like sandalwood for spirituality. Knead a few drops evenly into the clay or rub it into the wood/stone. (Hint: don't use a lot. The scent from essential oils is quite potent.) Then while you work, the oil's scent fills the air and your hands (which are in direct physical contact with the emerging pattern). The combination acts like aromatherapy to heighten your awareness and augment the magickal energy being created.

A Goal Mandala

Choose or make a mandala that represents an important goal in your life in manifested form. Make sure this figure inspires good feelings. (A symbol that evokes guilt or pressure won't be very productive.) Many people find that concentric circles around an image of the goal (a bullseye) or a cross in a circle with the goal superimposed on the X (like a target) work well. In this case X really does mark the spot! If you relate well to symbolic languages, add other dimensions like runes, magickal sigils, geomtrics, an affirmation, colors, etc.

Once you find or complete this figure, put it somewhere that you can see it regularly. Take ten to fifteen minutes out of each day to meditate while looking at that mandala. Let its pattern saturate your being. When the goal is reached successfully, burn or bury the mandala with thankfulness and make a new one!

Light Mandalas

I was walking through a toy store and noticed that they carried mandala-styled sun catchers (often fashioned after cathedral windows). As I looked at the sets, I realized that there was a powerful symbol here that I could use for magick: the sunshine pouring through the pattern represents fulfillment, enlightenment, and the universe's unfolding! I immediately bought one and enjoyed the activity so much that I wanted to offer it here as an idea for you too.

Since these were made for children, the instructions were wonderfully simple and the time necessary for creation brief (about an hour depending on how picky you are about your crafts). I was also delighted to discover that most sets had various colors to choose from, so you can color the mandala in a manner that suited your vision. When it is finished, hang it up in the window so the colors and light fill the room and your life.

For those of you reading this who enjoy sewing, there's an alternative for you to consider. Sew sheer fabric together in a mandala pattern that matches your goal (like a happy home) and then make this patch of fabric the center point in a set of curtains. If the adjoining fabric is heavy, the effect is even more profound when you hang them up. The backdrop remains dark while the center (the point) becomes a shining mandala that draws light and energy into the area where you most need it.

Name and Word Mandalas

These can be really fun to make. Let's start by looking at the name mandala. This can consist of your legal name or your magickal name. Work with your legal name if you've always had issues about it (such as not liking that name, or having changed it for some reason). Work with your magickal name if you want to direct energy toward your esoteric Path and its evolution.

Begin by writing your name as the outside edge of a large circle on the paper. You might have to write it several times to fill out this boundary. Now you have your name as the circumference of the mandala. This is the name people have known you by all your life, or the one by which people call you in the Circle. Ask yourself what that border represents to you.

You can now take this exercise in one of two directions. One approach is to fill in the mandala with images that come to mind when you think of your name. Start from the outer edge and work inward to get to the point. Let intuition guide you. Things close to the edge are generally peripherals—people or situations that somehow influence how you perceive your name, but often indirectly. As the images get closer to the point they become more intimate, those at the center representing the essence of your name and what it really means to you—how it's shaped who you are as a person.

The second approach requires filling in the mandala with words taken from your name, again using an inward spiralling pattern. If you think of this method like a word hunt puzzle it's easier. Look at all the letters in your name and think of smaller words that can be formed out of it. As you work, if other words or phrases come to mind don't shrug off that influence simply because it doesn't "fit" the pattern you've started here. You may need a new pattern, a new way of thinking. Since this mandala puzzle often awakens the intuitive nature, go with the flow!

The interpretive value of this second mandala works similarly to the first. The word or phrase that ends up at the center of your work will be the most revealing. Even so, pay attention to everything written around it. Like the mandala, we are the sum of our experiences, and those words are important. They fill out the circle that is you!

By the way, you can adapt this activity so that it focuses on a word or phrase instead of your name. For example, someone wishing to make a charm mandala might want to use the incantation for the charm as part of the mandala's construction. Since charms were often verbal or written, this maintains magickal congruity. When the words become part of the pattern they help to manifest the magick by design!

For example, say you wanted to make a mandala charm for prosperity. One way of doing this would be to begin with a green or gold circle (colors associated with money), with a dollar sign in the middle (the point of the activity). To "get to the point" in this case, you could create an inward spiral moving clockwise out of the words *"money to me, money to me, today I claim prosperity!"* Keep repeating the written words in the spiral until they reach the goal, then carry the charm with you until finances improve. At that point you can either burn the mandala to release its energy or give it to someone who has a need (hey, share the wealth!).

Auric Mandala

For this activity you'll need some private time for meditation and visualization, and paper and utensils for drawing. I suggest about an hour. I want you to find a place to get really relaxed and comfortable so you can turn your attention to your body's energy. If you feel tense, itchy, or self-conscious this activity won't work very well.

Now, extend your strong hand (the one you write with) about a foot away from your body. Close your eyes and breathe deeply. Extend your senses, paying particular attention to your hand. Slowly move the hand closer to your body until you feel a layer of heat-energy that might even seem to resist further movement down. This is where your aura lies. (This region changes with your mood, so don't always assume it will be in the same place if you try this activity more than once.)

Take your time and feel this energy as it lies in different parts of the body. Good checking points include your feet, knees, groin, stomach, chest, throat, forehead, and top of the head. Pay particular attention to any other sensual cues you get, like a smooth texture or a mental flash of color.

Turn your attention to the paper. Draw either the outline of a human body on the paper or a simple circle, which will represent *self*. This effectively is the boundary of your mandala now. Take your drawing implements and begin to express what you felt of your aura on that body or circle. Use color, geometrics, symbols, or whatever feels right.

When you're done, you can interpret your auric mandala using the keys in this chapter or the symbolic encyclopedia in Part 2. To those insights, also consider areas where the auric envelope wasn't even or smooth. Bulges, very thin auric coverings, rough auras, and the like often indicate emotional, physical, or spiritual dis-ease that needs to be rectified. If, on the other hand, you discover that a very healthy pattern emerges, consider carrying the completed mandala as a charm to continue manifesting wellness.

Group Mandalas

In Sanskrit one of the translations of the word mandala is "community" or "connection." One of the uses for mandalas is to allow people to think of one thing in terms of another and explore symbolic languages to express that relationship. This means that the mandala represents a way to reconnect with and better understand our tribes—that of family, friends, and even the greater community of humankind.

To make a group mandala, gather your tribe together and have each of them think of how they wish to represent themselves in the group mandala. Will they be a plant, a color, a shape, a number, a mineral, an animal, a rune? Will they be represented by a combination of symbolic elements that make up the whole person? Once that decision is made, each individual should make a small mandala using the emblems he or she has chosen.

Next, on a larger piece of paper (or something more permanent), make another large circle. This represents the whole group. Have each person place their mandala into that whole—where a person puts their piece is very telling. For example, someone who is the head of a household will often put their token near the center, representing his or her responsibility to act as the group's nucleus and cohesive core.

When the mandala within a mandala is completed, stand around it holding hands. Each person should take a turn explaining their personal mandala and his or her vision of what they bring to the family/group. They should also share their hopes for the future of that unit.

In the end, you may want to cover this with art spray and hang it somewhere that everyone can enjoy it. Consider making one each year so that the mandala grows and changes with the group that it represents.

Sensual Mandalas

For this activity I would like you to make five empty circles, each one of which has a different-colored rim (red, blue, yellow, green, silver, or another color of your choosing). These represent sight, taste, smell, touch, and hearing respectively. You will be working with one of these circles for an entire day, so that at the end of five days you will have completed all five.

Choose any one at random. Look at the circle (let's use sight's red circle as an example). Out loud say "I am conscious of seeing, within and without." Keep this phrase in mind all day and carry the circle with you. Pay particular attention to your sense of sight throughout your normal routine. If at any time you feel you want to draw something in the mandala that represents sight, do so. Otherwise wait and fill it in at the end of the day.

Continue over the next four days with the other four senses. Finally look over the mandalas you've made. Consider what you learned about yourself and how you use your senses from this activity. What sense appealed to you the most and had the strongest impact? This often indicates a personality element or something that's affecting you right now. For example, someone who is having communication problems might be strongly affected by the sense of taste (literally eating their words).

Edible Mandalas

As a wooden-spoon-wielding kitchen witch, I always try to find ways to apply magickal ideals to my cooking adventures. For mandalas, one way to do just that is by baking (or buying) an apple pie. The outer crust of the pie is your circle here, while the middle of the tin is the "point."

Before you put the pie in the oven (heat activates your magickal energy), make careful, precise, mandala-styled cuttings in the top of the crust, creating the pattern that you need. An apple pie is particularly suited to the goals of health and wholeness. Other kinds of pie can be considered for the esoteric value of the fruit.

Make sure to keep your goal in mind as you slice out the design. If you want to augment the energy further, recite a little mantra while the pie is in the oven. Finally, eat to internalize the energy!

In writing this chapter I found myself humming an old song (I can't recall the artist) that goes: *"the world is a circle that has no*

beginning and nobody knows where it really ends, and everything depends on where you are in the circle." How appropriate to mandalas, for this too is part of their lesson! The mandala embraces diversity—masculine/feminine, light/darkness, sound/silence. It is in many ways both a maze and a labyrinth, and yet neither. It reminds us also that so much of who we are and what we think depends on where we stand culturally, socially, and spiritually. Open yourself, open your heart, and open the circle! Let's get to the point together.

Maze, "Julian's Bower," Alkborough, Lincolnshire, circa 1675

4

MAZE: THE MIND'S DESIGN

What is this mighty labyrinth—the earth, but a wild maze
the moment of our birth?

—*British Magazine*, 1747, author unknown

"Keep your left hand on the wall." To get through a hedge, topiary, or stone maze without getting lost, this is the only instruction I'd ever heard about. Can this simple technique really resolve the riddle of the maze, or is there more to it? As I began to research this chapter, I discovered that this pat answer was only one part of a much more complicated pattern.

Sometimes called mazels or a mizmaze on the European continent, mazes have a lot in common with both mandalas and labyrinths. For contextual understanding, I'm going to make every effort to distinguish this pattern from the other two, but that's not as easy as it might sound. Sacred patterns are often connected, and understanding that connection is part of the magick. Nonetheless, to effectively use the maze pattern for magick we need to be able to recognize its earmarks—what makes it unique.

One difference between mazes, mandalas, and labyrinths can be seen in the way each pattern reveals itself. The labyrinth opens its truths a little at a time, making a subtle impression of its pattern on the seeker. During this process there is some sense of moving in and out, as if the labyrinth breathes with life and magick, but in the end the pattern always brings you to the point.

The mandala reveals its details from an examination of the whole. There is really nothing to solve here. The seeker's only task is making himself or herself aware of the pattern's parts, of the whole, and the interplay between the two. As this awareness grows it spins the magick and accentuates the point.

The maze, on the other hand, is very sneaky. It chooses to hide its point. A maze only reveals itself when someone is daring enough to challenge it, and cunning enough to see the design beyond the smokescreens. The reward for this effort is certainly worthwhile, however. Behind the illusion lies a pattern through which our magick can become reality!

A second telling difference between mazes, mandalas, and labyrinths are the questions each poses. The mandala asked: What's the point? The labyrinth asked: Do you want to pursue the point despite what seems to be? The maze complements both these inquiries by implying (through its complexity) that there are always new and different options, and other questions to ask! In this exacting setting, success isn't measured simply by moving forward or getting to the point, but by the way in which you choose to go through sheer ingenuity.

In this manner the maze is always evolving. You cannot see around corners, nor can you see the entire pattern until you look down on the maze or solve its riddle by deduction! A researcher and writer, Penelope Doob, explained this very neatly when she stated, *"[the maze] presumes a double perspective. Maze-treaders, whose vision ahead and behind is severely constricted and fragmented suffer confusion whereas maze viewers who see the pattern whole, from above or in a diagram, are dazzled by its complex artistry."*

All this sounds a lot like a metaphor for life, doesn't it? It should! Humans do not like chaos, but while we are in this maze called life things all too often seem chaotic. Juxtaposed against this confusion and multiplicity, we have the knowledge that life's maze has a center or resolution (self/spirit) and a unique order to it (call this fate or synchronicity). This knowledge helps drive us forward in the ongoing quest to claim our figurative brass ring, in this case personal fulfillment and spiritual enlightenment.

The reason mazes are so complex compared to labyrinths and mandalas is the fact that the pattern is multicursal, offering various paths, patterns, entrances, and exits, just as our daily reality does. This means that where the labyrinth's form and energy was distinctly feminine or "yin," the maze is the opposite. It accentuates "yang" rationality by appealing to and engaging the thinking mind—the part of us that's curious and likes a good mystery to unravel (hum, maybe we should bring Ariadne's Thread with us into this adventure too!).

The maze goes further than simply tempting us to engage it, however. Once within, it challenges the choice-making part of self. This is the part that makes moral and mundane decisions every moment of every day. It is the Priest, Priestess, or guru within—the voice of conscience, if you will, that must use rational processes to come to a resolution.

Now, most people who have listened to their inner voice know that it isn't always one hundred percent rational. Conscience, like it or not, also has instinctive leanings. Therefore, once we are mindfully walking or working with the maze, the activity can stimulate a cooperative venture between the intuitive self and conscious thought. When these two work together harmoniously they blend the best of the mandala and labyrinth together, resulting in a deep understanding of the mysteries and the self, stronger foundational skill sets, and the confidence to apply both—three things almost everyone would welcome!

As you review the history and examples in the rest of this chapter, keep your conscious mind at the ready. The maze teases our waking mind and wants it to work toward concrete understanding, even of those things that seem etheric. In this manner, the maze provides foundations when we're willing to work through its challenges. At the other side of successful completion, we find our answers to many of life's nagging questions.

A Myth-Adventure

Mazes aren't immune to myths, despite the fact that they're younger than labyrinths. One story in particular resonates with the maze's intriguing quality. It begins in England with King Henry II, who commissioned a topiary maze to be built at Woodstock.

In true royal fashion, this maze was an extravagant and gaudy effort probably designed to amuse the king more than anything else. Sounds straightforward enough, but that's not what bards of the time would have us think. According to the old songs and stories, King Henry used this complex weaving of greenery for an illicit purpose—that of keeping his mistress, Rosamund Clifford, hidden. She would go to the center of the maze awaiting the king's visit so Queen Eleanor wouldn't know about his frequent trysts!

Unfortunately (or fortunately, depending on your view), Eleanor was a wise and astute woman who knew of her husband's wandering eye. She also knew how to solve a maze. As you might guess, this means there's trouble brewing on the horizon for the king and his mistress. One day Eleanor sneaked quietly into the center and neatly killed her rival. From that day forward the maze received the name of Rosamund's Bower in the bard's stories, even though there are no physical signs that such a place ever existed!

It is an interesting aside, however, to learn that mazes were actually used during this era as secret meeting places specifically because of the privacy and safety they offered. No one but those given specific instructions could find the way to the meeting place! To this day, the maze still retains the symbolic value of confidentiality and concealment when we need those energies.

Making a Confidentiality Maze Amulet

Draw any maze as described in this chapter. In the center of the maze draw in words or symbolic images of the situation that you wish kept private. Afterward, choose a marker whose color represents confidentiality to you (some people like black because it creates a well-defined border). Trace the whole maze outline with this marker as you recite an incantation such as: *"What I place within, I bind within, it remains within. By my will this spell begins."*

Fold this maze in on itself three times and carry it with you until the need for secrecy has passed. Alternatively, wrap it around an object that represents the situation (like a business card for keeping a confidence at work) and keep it there until circumstances resolve themselves. At this point, burn the image with some incense to disperse its energy.

Another bit of lore surrounding mazes comes from England. According to regional superstitions, if you go to the center of a turf or earthworks maze on a summer's night (especially midsummer's night), you'll witness the things from which fables are made. You can catch a glimpse of fairies dancing!

This particular belief fascinates me in light of our earlier examination of both mandalas and labyrinths. Consider, for example, that the path of the labyrinth was often danced. So it seems our fairy friends are far more adept at maze navigation than we are, promenading through it rather than having to walk it cautiously. Then too, the center of the maze corresponds to the point of the mandala, which is a sacred place between the worlds—what better place for fairies to play? I'll be giving you some ideas on making your own fairy maze later in this chapter.

Finally, we come to a bit of information that mingles myth and history into an Ariadne-like clew for our consideration: the common folk name for mazes—Troy Towns. This intimates how difficult the maze is to solve by falling back on the infamy of Troy's defenses. History tells us that Troy had seven walls protecting it along with very intricate entryways designed to frustrate opposing forces.

Not surprisingly some early mazes had a seven-circuit design similar to labyrinths, basing this pattern on Troy's story. On a metaphorical level the maze makers hoped to improve the mazes' complexity by using this theme. It also confers the symbolic values of protection and safety on any maze that exhibits seven paths, seven entries/exits, or seven junctures.

Helpful Hint

Seven is a very magickal number. It can represent the colors of the rainbow, the days of the week, and the chakras. So, consider making a thematic maze based on any one of these three. Make sure the maze has seven different entries, exits, junctures, or threads and add suitable symbols into its making. As you do, pay particular attention to any of the junctures/threads that draw the attention of your conscious mind. For example, a day maze in which Tuesday's section comes out really well might indicate that Tuesday is a good day for your creative flow, or for working magick.

A-mazing Magick of the Maze

As you can tell already, mazes have a lot of allegorical value to ponder for our magickal pursuits. The first lesson that the maze teaches is the meaning and importance of the detours, setbacks, and delays that come up in our daily routine, and arise periodically on our spiritual path. It accomplishes this difficult task by purposely misleading the seeker with dead ends and alternative avenues that seem to serve no purpose. But these perceptions are deceiving. By discovering the "wrong" path we also eliminate an unproductive tact, and thereby improve our chances at successfully choosing a better course of action come the next attempt.

With this in mind, each detour and setback in the maze effectively becomes a Minotaur in our life's maze-labyrinth (remember the two patterns are intimately connected). This huge beast demands nothing less than tenacity and the ability to see various perspectives that we hadn't previously considered in order to be successful. While it is really the self being challenged, the maze becomes the *physical* obstacle that represents both the alternatives we're being offered and our doubts. To choose, we must confront and overthrow the shadow of uncertainty by learning to trust ourselves.

Now, let's put this into a more familiar spiritual context. Think back for a moment to the point in time when you first considered practicing magick. Didn't you feel a bit uncomfortable and uncertain? Didn't studying magick require a shift in your perspectives about the inner and outer worlds? Didn't you have to make amazing leaps of faith to begin believing the inherent magickal potential in the world and in yourself? Your initiation into magick was a very real Minotaur's lair. It was also a maze that you alone could solve for yourself.

I suspect that even experienced magickal practitioners still find themselves meeting challenges to that belief system—challenges that require some clearheaded thought to provide answers. I also surmise that nearly every truth-seeker faces moments of doubt about the verity of his or her mystical abilities and the value of the chosen Path—again two things that can be rectified with some sound, comparative thinking. Consequently, the decision to practice magick or any metaphysical belief system may be considered a type of a maze that drives home an important message: the rational mind plays an essential role in our spiritual pursuits!

Bet you didn't expect to read that last sentence in any book on magick, but it's quite true! Rational processes help us decide many things in our metaphysical practices, like what construct to use for a specific type of goal, what components are best to emphasize that goal, and most significantly, what path really makes us the best person we can possibly be.

The rational self also is the part that studies our art, that seeks out answers born from curiosity. This right-brained self yearns to uncover its magickal roots so as to build a secure spiritual foundation. Such foundations can't be built wholly by the left-minded dreamer and "witchful thinking." This substructure needs the concrete, logical, and sensible self as an architect. Mazes awaken that architect!

Beyond this, the maze offers the magickal practitioner two other bits of symbolism well worth considering. First, beneath all the mystery of the maze there exists a definitive, well-planned system that brings orderliness to what appears tumultuous. This order, while hidden at first, slowly unravels itself like Ariadne's Thread, offering us hope—a powerful motivator for magickal energy.

The Magickal Genesis Maze

For this activity I'd like you to make a list of all the people, ideas, or situations that once stood in the way of your decision to practice magick. Next to this list, create a symbol of that obstacle. Place those symbols anywhere you wish on any maze described in this chapter (or one of your own making).

Now, find your way through the maze with your finger. As you do, think about the manner in which you overcame each and every one of those barriers with time and patience. Solving this maze equates to the solutions you created for yourself long before you understood the power of patterns.

If you copy this maze and carry it regularly it can act as a powerful charm that gently reminds you of this truth: when you discover similar obstacles in the future, you always have the power within to leap them by using mind power and magick! You are your own architect.

Think about it for a moment. Would you even bother to cast a spell or meditate if you didn't truly hope for results? No! Such an act would seem, to your rational self, a waste of time. Nonetheless, the entropic nature of the maze shows us that even when we don't recognize a pattern, it still likely exists. Even when we don't see progress outwardly, it's likely occurring inwardly. This likelihood means that we have a very good reason to keep trying!

A Fun Project

Make a maze cover for your Book of Shadows. Allow the pattern to express both your magickal path (the intuitive) and the seriousness of your studies (the conscious mind). Use color, aromatics, and symbols in/on the maze to give it improved meaning. Also consider putting a word in the center of this maze that reflects your spiritual goals at this time. For example, if you're working on building confidence your word might be "faith" or "believe." This way the energy of the maze wraps around your Book of Shadows with the specific vibrations that you wish to inspire when reading it. (Reading is a function of the rational mind that's supported by the maze pattern.)

The second magickal maze symbol comes from its appearance. If observed from overhead, many mazes look like a knot or inter-woven pattern. Those of you who have been working magick for a while know that knot work and/or weaving is very impor-tant to spellcraft in that it can bind, release, braid, and/or blend energy into any abstract form.

By using the woven or knotted construct of the maze, we can tap the conscious, rational processes that give outward form, expression, and tangible substance to our magickal beliefs. Once this energy is tied into the pattern, in a typically maze-styled turn, it takes us back to the inception point. This is the mandala's point where we begin to comprehend or apply spiritual ideals in material ways.

The Knot Maze

While this is cheating a little bit, take a piece of tracing paper and copy some knot work from the Book of Kells, illustration shown on page 140.

Now, take a pencil, pen, or crayon whose color suits a specific magickal goal—but make it a goal that can be helped by mental effort on your part. A good example is improved focus for studying, maybe symbolized by red to draw your attention where it's most needed. Trace a path through the knotwork. In this case it doesn't matter if you cross over the same path twice (sometimes the way we arrive at knowledge is not direct). What's most important is that you keep your intention strongly in mind as you weave the solution into your maze. Carry this as a charm to support that goal magickally, and to remind you to remain an active participant in making this happen on a temporal level.

Finally, this brings us to a very effective application for mazes in magick: as images for pathworking exercises. The entire purpose of pathworking is to present an individual in a meditative state with a thematic landscape. While moving through this backdrop, the individual is given choices as to the progression of the activity, so a mazelike layout for the visualization is ideal. It allows the seeker to go where s/he wishes to go rationally (solving the personal riddle), and still leaves plenty of room for intuition.

It sometimes helps to show the person pathworking the basic pattern of the maze beforehand so s/he can better visualize it. Even so, if possible I suggest you forego this step with all but those people who have trouble conjuring up mental imagery. Why? Because the maze is illusive. Seeing it before the pathworking might influence the outcome of the exercise.

To give you an idea of how a maze-styled pathworking might go, here's a small sampling of one guide's words to a meditator. The purpose behind this particular pathworking is (a) allowing the participant to choose a plane on which to work (physical, etheric, mental) and then follow through on that choice by working through the maze symbolism provided by the guide.

To begin, the guide would wait until the meditator settled into a slow, rhythmic breathing pattern. When that person seems very relaxed and calm, the guide would begin speaking: "See yourself standing before a doorway that's open a crack. Just beyond the door you can see diffused, smoky golden-colored [yellow represents the rational energies of the maze] light . . . The light is warm and welcoming. It whispers to you to enter. Move up, push open the door, and walk through [pause for the meditator to reach the other side of the astral doorway]. As you look around you, notice that you're standing on a gently glowing brick walkway with hedges on both sides of you. Ahead the hedges branch out in three directions [body-mind-spirit]. Which path do you choose?" The guide waits for an answer and in this illustration would have three different maze patterns for the meditator to follow to expand on the theme s/he has chosen.

It's obvious that not all maze pathworkings focus on the physical, etheric, or mental planes. Any theme can be created that suits the maze pattern. Yet, because of the choices offered by the maze, the seeker can complete the pathworking with or without adhering to the focus for which the exercise was originally designed. Instead s/he will ultimately uncover the resolutionary path to the maze that s/he most need.

Momentous Mazes

Some researchers feel that mazes may have been developed as an ecclesiastical tool for prayer or penance because hedge and stone mazes often appear near, or on, Roman and Christian sacred sites. Other historians claim that the maze is a variation of a complex

Roman game played on horseback along a patterned route. I personally feel that mazes are more likely a younger cousin to the labyrinth, having evolved in complexity from that basic pattern when people wanted something both beautiful and challenging.

To modern minds, mazes are very different from mandalas and labyrinths because of the divergent symbolic value we see in these patterns. It wasn't always that way, however. Early writers frequently used the terms maze and labyrinth interchangeably, making it difficult to discern which was which in the old books without having a diagram or detailed written description.

We do know that the oldest documented maze (read: one that fits the multi-cursal description we now use) appeared in a Venetian physician's notebook in the late 1300s. This wasn't a great piece of art. In fact, it was much more like a random doodle, indicating a strong chance that the pattern was known long before then. Actually, many scholars feel that it's quite possible that Daedalus' labyrinth (discussed in the last chapter) was really a maze because of the highly complex system of hallways most accounts describe.

Just for Fun

Take the outline from one of the labyrinths in the last chapter that you particularly like and try to make it into a maze. To accomplish this you might have to add a few more courses, cut up the labyrinth and reassemble it differently, or place obstacles into various circuits that require directional changes to overcome them.

Alternatively, at various junctures in a large labyrinth pattern leave riddles that must be solved before the seeker moves on (the riddles equate to the Minotaur, the maze's dead ends, or its misleading paths). Either of these activities will give you a better feeling for how the labyrinth and maze are connected, and how one can reinforce or complement the other with a little ingenuity.

Confusing matters further, traditional mazes shared some common functions with labyrinths for quite some time. For example, mazes like Saffron on Walden were used for courting and marriage rites before they became objects of amusement. Similar to labyrinths, mazes were sometimes called Cities of Turnings, or *caerdroia* in Welsh. So, in exploring the history and symbolic value of the maze pattern, we should keep at least a snippet of labyrinth theories tucked into our proverbial pockets.

One interesting and distinctive function for some of the ancient mazes was that of a burial ground, such as in the Catacombs and elsewhere. While the Christian catacombs served a very practical purpose, there could have been other reasons for this type of burial structure too. First, a maze would help keep restless spirits trapped neatly within (as Daedalus' labyrinth-maze did to the Minotaur).

Remember, the ancients believed evil spirits didn't like going around corners. A maze to such a being would represent a tremendous challenge, and probably result in an astral headache. This means the spirits of the dead would not wander from the burial ground, and it also meant kindly spirits would be safe from malevolent influences so long as the body stayed on the hallowed ground. Additionally, and more sensibly, this configuration safeguarded the corpse from any would-be grave robbers! In both cases, however, the twists and turns of the maze seem to generate energies for safety.

Another interesting application for the maze was as a site for holding races. While one can certainly see the challenge in this, there was also intimation that whoever won the race would not only receive a reward but increase personal virility! This makes a little more sense when you consider that men ran most of these races, and the maze is considered aligned with active mas-

culine energies. Running the maze was also said to give power
to the sun, aiding it in its daily and annual cycle. This particular
connection will become clearer momentarily.

A third application for the maze is alluded to in the writings of
various historians who visited Wales. Mention is made several
times of the shepherds in this region cutting maze patterns into
fields. While this could have been a protective measure for the
herds considering the lore of mazes, it may also have some connections with sun worship. The pattern's creation, in this context,
could have been an act of worship or a kind of personal ritual. If
this is true, it strengthens the maze's association with the god
aspect, which is predominantly solar in the world's mythology,
and also explains why a maze race would be considered a type of
sympathetic magick to help the solar disk in its journeys.

By far, some of the most beautiful maze work seen throughout
global history was that grown in gardens. Nordic people may have
given birth to both garden and turf style mazes, not having the
stone necessary for other forms, but really this is only a theory.
For example, considering the description of the Gardens of Babylon, one might wonder if they didn't have a mazelike quality.

What we do know from the writings of diligent monks, historians, and naturalists alike is that hedge and topiary mazes
were often comprised of Yew, Cypress, Box, Laurel, Hornbeam,
Holly, Sycamore, Hawthorn, and Privet as foundational structure trees and bushes. (Green-thumbs take note!) These very
same writings indicate that the garden maze tradition began
around the twelfth century A.D. with Saxon herb gardens. When
planted near people's homes these little mazes translated into
elaborate kitchen gardens that were regularly harvested. (The
harvesting process helped maintain the overall shape and pattern of the maze!)

Shortly thereafter, the Dutch devised their own cultural twist
on hedge and garden mazes. Many of the turf mazes in this
region included a tree at the center. Some historians think this
alludes to an earlier pagan connection for this sacred pattern,

and I'm inclined to agree. The Germanic and Teutonic traditions both placed tremendous importance on the symbolic value of trees. They expressed this reverence in everything from the runes to calendar systems, so it would be perfectly fitting to bring that symbolic value into living mazes too.

A Simple Tree Maze

While it might sound terribly difficult to make a tree maze, you can create one with limited space, a potted decorative tree (like a hedge rose or weeping mulberry), and some crystals or tumbled small stones. Start by making sure your tree is in a large enough pot (or large enough section of soil outside) so the roots aren't compromised. Also make sure you have the right growing environment so it stays healthy. If the tree becomes sick, the magick in the maze also gets corrupted.

As you plant your tree, give it a name that reflects its purpose (whatever energy you're trying to grow and pattern from the maze). Be sure to remember this name as you will use it to address the tree whenever you tend it in the future. Then put the stones or crystals around the base of the tree in a mazelike pattern so that the tree's trunk becomes the center point.

Now, every time you water, weed, or fertilize, trace the pattern to the goal. This creates sympathetic energy with all the right designs to manifest that goal in reality, and with it you get a really happy, healthy tree besides!

Garden mazes reached a zenith with the Elizabethan knot garden, which was often filled with herbs and low shrubs for easy upkeep. In the sixteenth century a traveler would be hard pressed to find a German, Spanish, or English nobleman *without* a garden hedge, or topiary maze at his or her disposal (including Henry VIII). This style was equally popular in the Netherlands and France, and often included topiary pieces (animals or objects sculpted from shrubbery). Some of these mazes were done on such a grand scale that they became landmarks for seafaring vessels!

While all this hubbub was going on in Europe, Americans weren't taking very well to hedge mazes, even though maze motif could be seen in Native American rug designs. The settlers had little time for what they considered frivolous diversions; there were places to explore, land to develop, and fortunes to be made! Come the nineteenth century, however, the Industrial Revolution gave Americans a taste of leisure time, so hedge mazes started springing up on this side of the Atlantic. Writers of the era often mentioned, in true Victorian fashion, the pleasure of watching a village's young people playing elaborate games of peek-a-boo on May Day, and how it seemed as if an unseen presence was participating in the fun with them (similar to the English legends of fairies)!

Sadly, this upsurge in maze-making was temporary. Many gardens were neglected or lost during the two world wars. It wasn't until the 1970s that a new maze market was born on the heels of increased travel, tourism, and advertising industries. This market was not only evident in the United States, but extended itself into the Orient and countries where the maze had always been popular. In Britain alone, for example, it's estimated that about eighty mazes were built between 1980 and 1998.

With this history in mind, and the creative adaptations discussed below that modern mazes have experienced, the maze can become a magickal tool for:

- protecting self, objects, or areas. If you purposefully make or copy a maze on white paper (protective color) and wrap that paper around an object or carry it, the protective energy of the maze surrounds the object or goes with you.

- increasing courage, strength, or health. The solar nature of a maze, especially one depicted in yellow or gold (the sun's colors) acts as a natural amulet and charm for these goals.

- improving goal orientation, memory retention, comparative thought, and rational thought processes: Solving mazes regularly exercises your conscious mind and hones it.

- developing patience for trial-error scenarios: Mazes can be frustrating to make and work, but if you learn to give yourself time, you also can see how eliminating negatives eventually leads to the positives.

- honing directional senses: Within a maze, even one of your own devising, our sense of what constitutes the "right" direction is offset by the maze's clever disguise. By learning to see past that disguise, you teach yourself true-seeing!

- discerning simplicity in complexity: When you see a maze's solution it seems so easy, even if you struggled with it initially. This is the beauty of a maze—that beneath seeming convolution there lies a simple pattern for success.

- diagnosing the disposition of our lives: Do you keep running into the same wall in your life's maze? Are you moving backward in it or stalled altogether? Make a maze whose route and goal help you overcome these issues. (The pattern of the route and symbols at the goal help illustrate your need.)

- making decisions and/or coming to conclusions: If you think of the maze's goal as getting to the truth of a matter or as your final decision, and the route as the process, you can turn maze solving into problem solving in a meditative state.

- reawakening the inner child and a playful demeanor. Ultimately mazes are just plain fun, and if you make a growing maze out of fairy-friendly flowers, they will be even more so!

- cultivating a sense of adventure: as written in Goethe's Faust, "from point to point I float around, longing impatiently to break my glass and join the fullness of creation."

The point to point here are the options of the maze. The breaking of the glass is solving it or even exceeding the solution by seeing the maze in overview.

• weaving magickal energy for privacy or secrecy: The maze is a perfect symbol for this kind of energy. Add an image of one to the pages of your Book of Shadows!

I would like to stress that this list is my personal opinion only. Compared to mandalas and labyrinths, mazes are a relatively young spiritual tool. Consequently I've had to base my ideas on rather sketchy information assembled from a variety of folklore, relatively "modern" history, and sacred geometry. If you find the maze holds different meaning and potential for you, please trust that feeling and follow through on it. See where the magickal pattern of the maze leads you; let it unravel its mysteries in your mind and heart.

Modern Mazes

Studies have been done in modern times that show that focusing on mazes can help children calm down and better direct their energy. This came as no surprise to me after watching my daughter playing with the research books for this effort (in fact I had to fight with her a few times to get a peek at them!). She spent hours with a finger to a page, and was gleeful each time she solved the riddle presented. This is not the only way in which mazes are reappearing, however.

In Japan alone more than two hundred mazes have been built since the 1980s; Britain tripled the number of mazes it had, and other thematic ones appear every day ranging from the Darwinian Maze at Edinburgh Zoo and the Jersey Water Maze in the English Channel Islands (with water walls that constantly change) to the Worcester, England, maze that helps blind children develop sensory skills by providing a textural, audio, auric environment.

In Bath, England, the annual Bath Music Festival takes place in a maze. This maze has a key pattern made in marble mosaic. The overall images are of a river god, the seasons, the elements, and the rich Roman-Celtic history of this city. At the center there's also what's called a gaze made, which is solved visually. What's really wonderful is that this festival has a long-standing tradition that's helped to bring this maze into the public eye so its energy can be danced or just enjoyed for its beauty.

Tactile and Aromatic Mazes

Take two different mazes, one that you feel "looks" like it has a good pattern to represent the sense of touch (like a maze with a border that appears like an outstretched hand) and one that represents the sense of smell. On the first paper find all types of textures to adhere to it—feathers, small stones, sandpaper, glitter, fabrics, etc. On the other, dab various types of oils at different points in the maze. Put both of these away for about a week.

Now, take out the tactile maze and close your eyes. Move your finger over the surface and try to identify all the different textures. As you do, pay particular attention to the textures that appeal to you and those that don't. This mindful awareness can help you in other parts of magick—specifically in choosing the types of clothing you want to wear when working with different magickal themes.

Next, take out the aromatic maze and bring it close to you but not so close that the scents overwhelm. Now, try to differentiate between the aromas and also consider how they mingle together. Being more consciously aware of your scentual reactions will help you choose magickal incense and anointing oils more effectively!

While the maze's tradition has certainly been honored in recent years, the spirit, function, and appearance are also changing and evolving alongside the human creators. For example, portable mazes are being designed for a variety of special exhibits like community fund raising, earthwork mazes are being designed to augment spiritual energy, and scientists put animals in mazes to better understand nature's processes. Some individuals are making mazes in their back yards, others create them from cars in a parking lot or in corn fields, and others still make educational or sensory mazes for schools, and that's just the tip of the iceberg!

We have artists like Escher whose labyrinthian mazes astound us visually and intellectually. Then there's Adrian Fisher, the midwife to hundreds of modern mazes. He began designing mazes in 1975, many of which have variations on the labyrinth theme. Each one reflects a moment in history, the location in which it's placed somehow, or serves a specific purpose. For example, in 1993 Mr. Fisher created two celebrated mazes. One was a huge Stegosaurus maize-maze to benefit flood victims, which was unceremoniously disassembled after its use. The other maze helps teach blind people effective navigation methods to this day. You can learn more about Mr. Fisher and his work by accessing http://www.mazemaker.com.

Perhaps the neatest development in mazes are the games you can play at home. From maze pinball machines to ink-solvable maze books and other toys, the maze industry is alive and well. The rationally driven maze has even eked into computer technology via a program available called MAZE by Multimedia Software (203–256–5000). This software has good illustrations, includes the history and lore behind mazes, the ability to print many of the mazes, and a 3-D virtual maze. Note that the 3-D section isn't really fancy graphically, and may leave the spoiled media tycoon somewhat flat, but for anyone interested in a ready reference it's worthwhile.

Solving the Maze's Riddles

An eighteenth-century designer of labyrinths by the name of Batty Langley explains the purpose of mazes as this: "To require an intricate and difficult labor to find out the centre, and to be so intricate as to lose one's self therein and to meet with as great a number of stops therein and disappointments as possible." I might hazard to add that in losing one's self on the maze's highway and byways, perhaps we are also finding ourself by reaching out with our minds in new and different ways.

Be that as it may, in deconstructing the maze, we need to bear in mind that not all of them can be untangled by applying the "hand on the wall" trick (keeping one hand on a wall at all times). If the maze has a single interconnected border, that will work and eventually lead you into the center. If the maze has unconnected segments, which is often the case in more contemporary creations, that technique will likely take you round in circles! So our modern maze makers have tested the rational mind even further by eliminating a "given."

A couple of mazes I came across had a very unique solution to them. The exit was actually the same as the entrance, even though the path never backtracked or crossed along the way. To me, this has very strong symbolic value about how our past is always with us, touching our thoughts and perceptions today.

Following is a list of some other traditional maze symbolism. Unfortunately this list is limited by the shorter history of the maze, and the lack of extended studies on its spiritual value. To help fill in the gaps, you may be able to apply the color and shape values from the labyrinth correspondences here because of the similarities between these two patterns. Just bear in mind that the labyrinth associations will exhibit a stronger rational energy when placed into a maze. For example, if you were to choose colors and patterns for love and place them into a maze, this would augment your ability to think clearly about a relationship rather than amplifying romantic tendencies.

Maze Correspondences

- center: the intuitive, yet guided by reason; a specific goal or idea toward which you're working

- complex patterns: the intricacy of close relationships or intimate situations
- cupid ornaments: a love maze (note where cupid's arrow is pointed; this can be very telling if your attention is in the wrong place)
- exterior, periphery lines: the linear world
- high walls: privacy, challenges, intimacy, trust
- intersection: the meeting of two paths, two options. A place where you can bury the past and build toward the future. This can also indicate an energy vortex in larger maze efforts
- low walls: open demeanor; receptivity; easing constraints
- outside (beyond the walls): external sources; the environment and people around you. This region is particularly telling in spontaneous maze drawings
- spirals: defenselessness; going around in circles
- tree center: the tree of self; our connection to nature; pay particular attention to the condition of the tree in spontaneous activities for more insights
- winding paths: the difficult road to salvation or enlightenment

As you can see, this list still leaves a lot of questions. So the elusive nature of mazes remains, taunting and teasing our consciousness. Every route, curve, detour, entry, and exit represents a choice to make in order to solve the mystery ahead. This design means that the maze's pattern keeps shifting, transforming, and evolving in much the same way a seeker's perceptions and perspectives should transform and evolve from the exercise.

Walking the Maze

In considering which of the aforementioned patterns, or alternatives, to use in your own maze activities, you may wish to

ponder an observation made by a seventeenth-century writer
by the name of Dr. Harris. In his studies, Dr. Harris uses the
words maze and wilderness interchangeably, and concludes that
the maze can be very allegorical. So what wilderness do you
want to explore or transform? What allegory do you wish to
unravel and comprehend? The options are only limited by what
your rational mind can accept as valid.

A second consideration in your maze activities is whether or
not you want to adapt the ideas you liked from the mandala
and labyrinth chapters to the maze motif. Since these three patterns intertwine, there's no reason that you couldn't use some of
the modes and methods from the previous two. The only caution is to make changes to those media that better suit the
maze's distinct magick.

For example, at the outset of this chapter we talked about
how the maze challenges our thought process. So, you might
adapt the mandala's mantra-reciting technique here for maze
walking by simply changing the phrase to something like: "I
think, therefore I am!" The "I am" portion reconnects mazes to
their distant cousin the mandala, and provides a more intuitive
balance to the rational "I think."

Whether or not you use mantras, however, there are still
three more things to consider before creating your maze-walking
efforts:

1. Where do you want the "goal" to be? Unlike the mandala
   and labyrinth, a maze's solution doesn't have to be in the
   middle. It could be at the end or exit, or anywhere else
   you choose to hide it. Bear in mind the symbolic value of
   this placement, such as putting the goal in the east to generate hope in your daily thoughts, or in the southern part
   of the maze to create intense mental energy.

2. Do you want to put personally significant objects or imagery
   at various junctures of the maze, or at the goal point? This
   helps to blend your intuitive self with the rational self by
   appealing to our innate reactions to symbolic languages.

3. How much time do you have to spend on upkeep? People with hectic schedules will not want to make a maize maze or hedge maze simply because they require hours of tenacious care to maintain. Meanwhile charm mazes, window-box mazes, and other media presented in chapter 1 do not require tons of time, and still allow you to "walk" the maze in various forms.

It's interesting to note that people who have walked large mazes often report that it's in the moment they give up and attempt to return to the beginning that the maze is solved. Unwittingly they find themselves in the middle because of turning themselves around. I think this gives us something important to consider. Is the way to solving the enigmas in our lives simply a matter of turning things around and looking at them differently? Very frequently the answer is *yes!*

Mazes on Your Mind?

If you have a dream about mazes, which may very well happen when you're working on one subject so intensely, this dream can mean various things. From a purely pragmatic standpoint it might indicate that you need to take a break from the subject. Perhaps your dream is offering a different perspective about the magick of the maze that you hadn't previously recognized.

Now, I know that after reading this last paragraph some readers will say, "but the maze works with the conscious/rational mind, and dreams come from the subconscious." Yes, that's true, but conscious rational things have a way of leaking into the depths of our spirit too. The subconscious then wrangles with the information and presents it to us in a different form while we're more receptive—namely during sleep!

From various tomes on dream interpretation here are some of the ways of interpreting a maze-themed dream:

- Indecision: since the maze challenges our choice-making self, seeing one in a dream may indicate the inability to choose between equally appealing options, or vacillating on an important choice.

- Entanglement: mazes can also symbolize confusing or intricate situations in an environment where you spend a lot of time. Either untangle Ariadne's Thread, get away from unhealthy circumstances, or consider if this is a situation in which you should even involve yourself.

- A maze at night may presage troubles, often of a physical or mental nature.

- A turf or topiary maze is often considered a positive omen for relationships and specific projects.

- Several mazes networked together may signal oncoming troubles with travel.

- Solution: review the pattern of the maze for a symbolic answer to your problems.

- Overcomplicating simple matters. Return to the beginning and streamline!

- Trickery: since the maze plays with our senses it may well be that someone is trying to alter your perceptions of the truth.

- The need for order and symmetry. Something in your life is in disarray. Put your house in order.

This list can apply to seeing a labyrinth in dreams too, but you should interpret the latter on a more figurative/intuitive level. And, as with all types of dream interpretation this is a subjective list that depends greatly on other factors in your dreams including colors, objects, sounds, textures, words, and imagery around the maze. Take into consideration all the parts of your dream maze to best understand what it's telling you.

Sample Maze Activities

As with mandalas and labyrinths you can plan your mazes or make them spontaneously. However, I think the construct of the maze lends itself far more effectively to the planned activities.

Having said that, please don't forget that maze walking can be very playful too. It seems to create an atmosphere of sportive revelry. This comes directly from the maze's original personality, since many early mazes were created for pure enjoyment.

So if you need to remind yourself of the value of play, or reconnect with your inner child, both are perfectly fitting applications for its pattern despite the cognitive construct. To achieve this, simply enter into a maze-walking activity with no other goal than sheer pleasure and enjoy! Here are some other ideas upon which to base your maze-walking activities:

The Fairy Ring Maze

Garden mazes in particular offer plenty of room for adding symbolic value to the route via flowers, plants, trees, statuaries, and the like. In keeping with the English lore shared earlier, this particular garden maze is meant to attract the wee folk to your home or windowsill greenery. To create it you'll need a circular area of good soil that gets exposed to both light and shade daily. Depending on how much room you have, you'll want to collect healthy specimens of any of the following plants: hawthorn, primrose, rosemary, thyme, clover, and oak, all of which are traditionally favored fairy hiding spots. You may also want to get a fairy cross (the stone staurolite) to use as decoration or place in the soil, some sweetbread, tiny bells, and a chair or two from children's doll houses (other things that fairies are said to like).

Once you have everything together, wait for a full moon to plant your garden. This is not only the best time to sow most greenery for lushness, but also the time when fairies are most active. Other timing considerations that appeal to the fey include: the hour of midnight, midsummer's night, lammas (August 1), and Halloween. While you're waiting for a suitable day and time, find or make a maze pattern that you think is whimsical enough (and difficult enough) to appeal to these playful creatures.

Finally, set your plants in the ground with natural fertilizer.

Sow them clockwise through the maze pattern you've designed to generate positive energy. Afterward make sure to spend some time in or near the garden so you can get a peek at any spirits who come a-calling!

Beach Maze

Instead of making a sand mandala as we talked about in Chapter 2, this activity centers around making a beach-front maze. Above and beyond any complexity you put into the maze, there are two additional challenges here: creating and solving the maze before the tide washes it away! So you'll want to check on the time for high and low tides and make sure you begin your efforts when there's enough time to complete them.

You'll want to pick a stretch of beach where your maze creation won't be disturbed until it's done. I strongly suggest checking with a lifeguard or other beach authority to make sure you can do this without getting in trouble. If you tell them that other beach visitors can try the maze when it's finished, I think you'll meet with great success and support.

As you etch out the maze in the sand, keep in mind its ultimate purpose. In effect, you're representing your will and conscious aims with each line created. Later on, the sea will carry away this energy to the entire world!

By the way, if you'd like to add another symbolic dimension to your beach maze, consider creating it when the tide-time augments the magick you're devising. The Norse people gave each arriving tide special significance. So, if you know that a tide is going to arrive first thing in the morning, which is a symbol of alertness and vitality—it would be something very suited to maze-making and walking!

Day tides represent financial improvements and maturity (personal or the fulfillment of a project), midday tides represent will and determination, and pre-dusk tides are symbolic of keen perception, so this is a good time to create a maze where you want to improve your perspective. The evening tide flows in with a spiritual focus to balance the conscious energies of the maze. It also supports the playful, joyful nature of this pattern. Night tides are best suited for contemplating difficult subjects, the midnight tide helps with physical matters, and pre-morning tides stress silent introspection.

Student's Maze

We've already talked in depth about how the maze's pattern stresses focus. So if you're having trouble with your studies in a particular subject, you may want to consider making a maze book cover to provide some magickal help. First, consider the subject itself. How can you represent it in the maze? I suggest putting the symbol you choose in the middle of the maze because that's your "point"—the goal toward which you want to direct your mind and will. This also means that you'll have to use a maze pattern whose goal lies at the center of the maze instead of elsewhere for best results.

Put your maze on a yellow background (yellow augments the mental plane because it's the color of the sun). Whenever you feel yourself getting distracted, trace the maze pattern to the center with your finger. This visually and metaphorically brings you back on track!

Office Maze

Building on the idea presented in the student's maze, who of us couldn't use a little more focus at work? The hard part here is figuring out the best way to create your maze so it represents your job, and then where to display it so you can see and use it regularly. A secretary, for example, might make a maze with a pencil or telephone in the middle and put it on her typing stand. A construction worker might make a maze with a hammer in the center and put it on his tool box. In both cases, when the person feels daydreams and other diversions turning attention to things other than work, they trace the pattern to turn the focus back where it belongs.

Magnetic Maze

To create a magnetic maze, you'll need a thin wooden box (like plywood) and several smaller pieces of wood with which to create your maze pattern. You'll also need a lead ball and a large magnet. Alternative materials for this project are a flat metal surface, wood slices with magnetic strips on one edge, the lead ball, and a magnet.

For the first maze, you need to be fairly adept at woodworking since you'll need to nail or glue each slice of wood into the box in the maze pattern desired. The alternative is a little easier. By placing a magnetic strip along the thin, bottom edge of each wood slice you can arrange them any way you wish on the metal surface. You won't get frustrated when a piece doesn't get nailed in correctly because you can always move it! Better still, this option allows you to re-use the materials for different types of mazes whereas the first maze box is permanent.

Once you've patterned out the wood slices in either of these two projects, place the lead ball at the beginning spot. Use your magnet to draw the ball through the maze's energy, neatly attracting whatever magick you've designed toward the "goal" and manifestation. Then carry the ball with you as a charm to keep the magick "rolling."

Maize Maze

I spoke earlier in this chapter about people who use corn fields for making large walkable mazes (think of crop circles with an attitude!). Now, since most folks I know don't live anywhere near a corn field, there might be another way to make a maize maze out of popcorn or cooked yellow corn. In both cases you can create a maze pattern that represents financial abundance or providence, then eat it afterward to internalize your magick!

Taking this idea one step further, you can buy colored unpopped popcorn at many supermarkets. This might make a good medium for charms, amulets, and talismans if you lay out a pattern and glue the kernels to paper or cloth. Choose the order of the kernels by their color so that the hues harmonize with the goal of your maze. Using the previous example, you might choose predominantly green kernels for money magick.

Tea Garden Maze

A much more elaborate maze, the idea for this comes from the Victorian era. Basically you'll need a yard in which you can design a stone or herb maze in such a manner so that the center of the maze has a table and chairs for tea. Why have tea time in the middle of a maze? Well, what better "point" could be designed as a private place for people to discuss all manner of rational thoughts?

Here's a list from which to choose some of the stones and herbs for your tea garden maze. Each of these metaphysically improves mental keenness and cordial communications:

celery	periwinkle	rosemary
lily of the valley	savory	mints
mustard	sweet pea	lavender
meadowsweet	violet	iris
sage	agate	carnelian
bloodstone	beryl	

Along with your choice of plants and stones you may want to add a set of windchimes. Bells are protective, and the air element motivates positive conversation. Or consider patterning the maze like a spider's web with the tea table in the center (in Native American tradition spiders created language and writing).

As with all patterns, the actual layout of this garden is wholly personal and difficult to dictate in this book because I don't know how much room you have. For example, people who don't have lawns might choose to grow some herbs in patterned flower pots near the areas where you converse regularly.

Maze Amulets

Any time you feel as if you're under psychic or mental attacks, find a very complicated maze pattern. Bless this by repeating an incantation like this one seven times: "Corners you cannot go around, by my will all evil's bound. Within this maze that turns and winds, all negativity I now bind!" Carry this with you until the problems seem to abate. At this point you should burn or bury the amulet to disperse the bad vibes it collected.

Some Afterthoughts

The center of a consecrated maze becomes a sacred space—it becomes the mandala because it represents the solution. When the maze is solved rationally it becomes a labyrinth—with but one true path that's sure. This opens the way for the intuitive self to venture forth. When the labyrinth is completed using this intuitive nature as a guide, like a mobius strip, it becomes the mandala: the prototype for wholeness.

In this manner, these three emblems seem to constantly touch on one another and influence one another. Together they combine yin with yang, god with goddess, and become a reflective surface for our soul. In this powerful mirror we discover, or are gently reminded, that human beings are indeed far more than the sum of our parts and patterns. We are special, we are unique, we are divine, and we are the magick!

From the Book of Kells, circa 900 A.D.

PART TWO

MAGICKAL MOTIFS

I on thy path O god, thou O god in my steps
—Gaelic charm

USING THE ENCYCLOPEDIA

We (the Sioux) see in the world around us many symbols
that teach us the meaning of life. . . . You could notice if
you wanted to, but you are usually too busy. We Indians
live in a world of symbols and images where the spiritual
and commonplace are one.

—Lame Deer, *Seeker of Visions*

Lame Deer's wisdom shows that there are literally thousands
of sacred patterns, sigils, and symbols in the world to consider
for a book of this nature. Any one of these thousands could
become part of the base motif for labyrinthian spells, visualizations, gardens, maze rituals, magickal home decor, and much
more. I must confess that the variety and beauty of many of
these designs made it difficult to decide among them!

Even so, I've tried to limit this study to those patterns that I
felt would be most useful to your labyrinth-walking activities
no matter what basic form they take (see Chapter 1). Among
them I've included shape, numeric, and color correspondences
so that you can consider these factors in interpreting spontaneous patterns or in making ones for a particular purpose. Please
know, however, that this list should in no way hinder your creativity in labyrinth-walking activities. If you feel like using a
design that doesn't appear here, by all means do so! And if you

feel a design means something other than what's described here, always trust yourself over any book.

As you review these entries you'll also notice that animal correspondences appear. Some people reading this may say, "I can't possibly draw an animal, so how can I use these characters?" Since I number myself with the artistically challenged, I've come up with two solutions to this quandary that work for me and may help you too. First, you could just draw *part* of the animal or a symbolic depiction of it. In magickal patterning the symbol is every bit as potent as what it represents. Second, you could find a picture or photograph of the animal, or look for a snippet of fur, a found feather, and the like from it in a natural setting. Then all you have to do is CPA (cut, paste, and assemble)!

Along the same lines, there is absolutely no reason why a labyrinth activity couldn't use any number of other media: ribbons, buttons, photographs, glitter, cutouts from cards, wax drippings, finger paints, tiny shells, tumbled crystals, and the like. This approach allows you to bring a textural appeal to the whole and gives the final product more depth than a simple drawing can render. It's also fun, and a good spiritual activity for children. From my own experience I can confidently say that parents will learn a lot about their kids this way.

Finally, as you read the encyclopedia, beginning on page 148, bear in mind this seven-step process for creating your sacred patterns. It easily applies to any planned labyrinth-walking activity you wish to undertake, and even has some bearing on spontaneous creations:

1. **Be still.** Sacredness is generated in part by stillness—by quieting our minds and souls long enough to hear the Divine speaking, or hear our own wise, intuitive voice from deep within. Stillness also, by its nature, generates a magickal, prayerful state of being. Between each breath is stillness. Between thought and action . . . between world and not-world lies stillness. And in that brief moment of waiting, an

attitude is born that is more open to connecting with and receiving from Spirit as well as your own higher self.

2. **Be patient. Wait for inspiration.** This ties directly into stillness. Patterns can't be rushed or coerced; they just don't work that way. Oh sure, you can try, but a pattern born out of inspiration will be far more potent than one forcibly eked out (if the latter works at all). Remember, all things in their right time. If now isn't the right time, wait. You will know when the moment is most propitious.

Seven Steps for Planning Sacred Patterns

1. Be still
2. Wait for a glimmer of inspiration
3. Determine the goal
4. Decide how to get to the point
5. Consciously decide to follow through
6. Make the pattern
7. Use the pattern to manifest your magick

---

3. **Determine your goal.** There's a very good possibility that you began this whole activity knowing what the goal was, but if you suddenly realize there's something else that requires your attention, now's the time to reconsider your approach. If you didn't have a particular purpose in mind, you should consider finding one. Labyrinth walking is generally most effective when you're moving toward a specific point.

The exception to this rule is when the "point" is to try and unlock or uncover something whose source isn't certain, like understanding the basis of an irrational fear.

While the goal of this activity is obviously understanding, you don't know the root of the fear, so it would be difficult (and possibly detrimental) to design the labyrinth activity around that fear. In this case you'll want to leave the point of your pattern open, and let that originating circumstance reveal itself to you through the exercise.

4. **Decide how to get to the point.** Look at the three motifs (mazes, mandalas, and labyrinths). Which motif, and which application of medium, is best suited to the need at hand? Each of these motifs lists some spiritual applications to which it has been applied in its respective chapter. If you can find something similar to your goal in that list, you've got a great starting point.

   In terms of application, bear in mind that while moving through the labyrinth is always a good activity, it's not always suited to our circumstances or needs. For example, one wouldn't lay a huge cloth mandala down at work to walk it for inner fortitude for obvious reasons. On the other hand, you could make a small mandala charm and put it under your desk or chair instead. Review the applications in Chapter 1 to determine which one seems most suited to your need or goal and feels right considering the situation at hand.

   This is also the point at which you should be reviewing the symbols here or in other books you may have. Which ones give you an immediate "Ah, ha!" reaction when you're thinking of the magick you hope to create? Pick a few and use these for the starting point of your patterned activity. Note, however, that they are starting points only. Where your creativity and Spirit take you from there is wholly up to you.

5. **Consciously commit yourself to following through.** At this point there's a temptation to put aside the books and mentally file the information gathered and come back to it later. You can do that if necessary, but *do* come back to

it! You've started to weave an energy pattern by acting on the first four steps of this process. Don't leave those psychic threads just hanging in the air. Do something with them!

6. **Make the pattern.** Create your pattern in whatever way suits your chosen application. Again, let your instincts guide you. Labyrinth walking is all about facing and trusting yourself, so don't get so caught up in *how* you're making the pattern that you forget *why*.

   Similarly, please don't focus so much on the pattern you've chosen that you overlook the voice of Spirit or your superconscious urging changes. The process of designing and walking your labyrinths is, in itself, a labyrinth—you have to balance head and heart, and listen to both for the greatest amount of success.

7. **Manifest the pattern.** Follow up your labyrinth-walking activities with thoughtful, concrete gestures. When the magickal work is done, it's time to act—to keep the energy in motion—to give your magick a place in which to take root. Don't create a sacred pattern then sit back and expect the universe to do all the work for you. It simply won't happen. Instead, become a proactive co-pilot in designing your destiny. Get out and do everything possible on a temporal level to help the magick along . . . to live the pattern in word and deed.

This seven-step process has been very effective for almost everyone who tried it. The key for each attempt was having a strong belief in the pattern and application, and trusting the self. Faith can move mountains when it's supported by confidence, willpower, and a heartfelt vision of the Sacred energies. So be prepared to move and shake a few mountains!

ENCYCLOPEDIA OF EMBLEMS, SIGILS, AND SYMBOLS

We could not include illustrations of these items in a book of this size. If you're looking for good pictoral references, please refer to texts like Barbara Walker's *Women's Dictionary of Symbols and Sacred Objects,* James Wasserman's *Art and Symbols of the Occult* and Miranda Bruce-Mitford's *Illustrated Book of Signs and Symbols* for assistance.

Abracadabra The most famous magickal word known, the gnostics and Hebrews used this to banish sickness by writing it in the form of a descending triangle. It's actually thought that the term means "to perish like the word" so it's the perfect image for diminishing problems of any sort. To make this into an effective labyrinth-walking tool, it might be laid out in a downward-pointing triangle. Then paths can be laid into the triangle between the letters. An individual walks back and forth from the top down to the bottom, following the shortening pattern to create personal wellness.

There is no reason not to use the form of this amuletic device and change the word so that it's something more personally meaningful. You can also reverse the form (point-up triangle) and the walking pattern (from the point to the base) to create positive energy rather than banishing.

Almond shape Traditionally called a mandorla, this is the shape of a halo that denotes spiritual energy. It's also considered feminine in nature.

Anchor Safety, stability and foundations (even in figurative rough water).

Androgyne A bisected diamond, this symbol was used in old Christian sects as a Western version of the yin–yang (mandala) and balance between these two basic forces in the universe, let alone ourselves.

Ankh An ancient Egyptian symbol of stability, long life, and durability. The word ankh means "life" and the symbol looks much like a sandal strap, implying the soul's freedom to walk and move in life and the next as a citizen of eternity.

Ant Using the image of an ant in your labyrinth-walking effort denotes orderliness (maze), cooperation, and community.

Arrow Direction and guidance; hitting the "point" (mandala). Three arrows bound together is a traditional symbol of unity, the trinity, and virility.

Aum In various mystery schools this word/sound is part of the creative language that brought all things into physical reality. It represents spontaneous manifestation.

Axe An ancient symbol of Zeus, this represents power, justice, authority, and learning life's lessons.

Basket Abundance and fruition.

Bear The bear represents a specific phase in your life, a time of hibernation or self-imposed hermitage that's either beginning or ending. Also, in shamanic traditions the bear is often a means of communicating with and moving between the worlds. If you've had out-of-body experiences, started sensing spirits, or felt that astral travel was something you should try, a bear showing up in a spontaneous effort would indicate you're on the right track.

Bell The shape of a bell is usually associated with the goddess, whereas the ringing of a bell in your labyrinth-walking activities can signal the start of sacred space, emphasize harmony, and generate protection.

Binah The number three in the Kabbalistic tree of life that invokes understanding and comprehension, and also helps us communicate that knowledge effectively.

Birds Like many winged creatures, birds often represent the soul in flight or spiritual movement. A lot here depends on whether it appears if the bird is moving up or down. A bird moving up could symbolize spiritual growth or ascension. One flying down toward the point of a mandala could portend heavenly aid or guidance from the Ancestors.

As with all animals, each type of bird has a specific meaning. Here's a brief list of aviary correspondences:

- crane: messages from the divine; enlightenment; wisdom
- crows: bearers of omens and signs
- dove: peace; spiritual gifts; understanding; piety
- duck: contentment; fidelity; renewal
- falcon: god aspect; strength; liberation
- goose: good news
- hen: maternal nature
- hummingbird: truth; beauty; harmony; pleasure
- kingfisher: marital bliss; magick
- parrot: imitative magick; love; prophesy
- peacock: watchfulness
- robin: compassion
- rooster: hope; victory; vigilance
- sparrow: solitude; loyalty
- swallow: renewal; cycles
- swan: self images; beauty; trust
- woodpecker: luck; magick

I suspect drawing different species will be difficult for most readers, so if you want to use the symbolism, I suggest either finding a feather for that bird and carrying it as a charm, or using a cut-out image from a nature magazine instead.

Black Many creation myths, including that of the Maori, begin with darkness to which light suddenly comes. This transformation is an alchemical shift, denoting potential that exists even in what appears to be nothingness. These stories also indicate that black is a very primal color, representing both life and death (the womb and grave), the earth and sky (dirt and night's blackness). It also symbolizes those things that go beyond our normal senses, the expanse of time, and the negatives with which one grapples.

Slowly going over a black labyrinth pattern with white (or another upbeat color) is one way of repatterning negativity with more positive energies. To augment black's overall vibrations use it in patterns with eight points or courses, or work on a Saturday.

Blue This color implies peace and serenity. In Native American tradition it represents honest intentions, while in Jungian philosophy it symbolizes the "as above so below" axiom of Wicca (the vastness of the sky, the vastness of the ocean). In Christianity it is a feminine hue that's often associated with Mary and therefore the goddess.

Blue is also the color of compassion, of returning to the source of our beginnings, and by so doing, awakening our empathic self. In esoteric tradition it corresponds to the throat chakra, meaning any pattern focused on finding one's voice or improving communication skills should have some blue highlights. To improve blue's effect, use it in patterns bearing six segments or work on a Friday.

Box A box is a three-dimensional square or rectangle and can have similar connotations. Because of the story of Pandora, consider wisely what you wish to place in the box, or what you choose to release from it. Boxes (with tokens within) make a fun tool for maze work, or as a surprise waiting in the center of the labyrinth for successful seekers.

Bridge A pathway between the worlds or a way around an obstacle. Bridges are often used in full-scale labyrinths and mazes at transition or decision-making points to accent that energy.

Broom In some magickal groups the labyrinth pattern is brushed with a broom prior to walking to invoke blessings and banish any random energies that might hinder the activity.

Bull The bull is a lunar animal that may represent a need to reconnect with your intuitive nature. In Babylonian tradition it represents strength, virility, and might. Also, because of modern language it can symbolize being overly stubborn, or the need to take control of a situation especially when it appears in spontaneous exercises.

Butterfly Among nature's most beautiful emblems of transformation, the butterfly is also associated with our psychic nature. In mandalas in particular a butterfly's appearance can announce Spiritual renewal or a fresh beginning.

In other pattern work, a butterfly is an excellent emblem to choose for manifesting your dreams in reality. This will require a lot of work on your part (butterflies weave their own transformation chambers), but the effort is well worth it!

Caduceus I think this image would make for a really interesting maze or labyrinth motif where the two mouths of the snakes are the entries or exits. Because the Mesopotamians and Greeks both associated this emblem with healing, and the symbolism remains to this day, consider adding this image to your patterns for health and overall wellness in body, mind, or spirit.

Candle Walking a labyrinth or maze, and making mandalas by candlelight can be a very interesting experience compared to normal lighting. Candles accentuate the spiritual nature and have a gentle glow that helps us tap into our intuitive self.

Chesed The number four in the Kabbalistic tree of life that represents earth and foundations (ideas taking their place in concrete reality; magick becoming matter). A variant spelling is Hesed, meaning mercy.

Chokmah or **Chochmah** The number two in the Kabbalistic tree of life where the point becomes the line around the mandala or the path of the labyrinth. This defines the point and helps us distinguish what is what (and who is who). Chokmah is a measure and guide that helps manifest wisdom.

Circle One of the most important symbols in human consciousness, circles represent protection and the delineation between the worlds. In magick, the circle is a safe place for worship and celebrating the eternal nature of soul. In mandalas, the circumference of the circle is essential to understanding and integrating the whole portrait.

Use circles in your patterning work when you need to compare, recognize, or generate synchronicity. Add them to labyrinths where you seek to find unity without sacrificing diversity. Circular mazes, on the other hand, are one way of balancing the intuitive (circular) with the rational (maze) mind.

Collar In Egyptian tradition a golden collar was placed on the necks of important mummies to ensure them of freedom from all fetters in eternity. Adapting this a bit to our labyrinth-walking activities, I'd suggest if you're wearing a collar, loosen it! Liberate yourself from ties to the mundane world for a few moments.

Compass Many mazes and labyrinths were aligned somehow with the compass points, and some even included a compass layout within. This most likely symbolizes the four corners of creation and the energies each houses.

Cornucopia This represents fertility, plenty, and providence. It would make a really neat pattern for the unwinding path of a labyrinth.

Crescent A sacred pattern to the Turkish, Arabian, and Abyssinian people, this usually represents the moon. The most common applications were for strength, protection, and to turn away the influence of the evil eye.

Cross While most people are familiar with the Christian connotations for the cross, it is a very old symbol that often represented the four corners of creation, the four directions, and four winds. Because it also looks like an X, a cross-pattern in labyrinth walking can also indicate conjunctions, connections, choices, and the meeting place between worlds. In this case, X truly does mark the spot!

There are many styles of cross (see also Tau Cross). The Etoile cross invokes the elements, the patee cross is sacred to Frey, the pomme cross symbolizes the four major festivals of the year, as does the solar swastika which has a cross motif. The interlaced cross shows how the lower and upper worlds (the inner and outer) are forever joined, the lunate cross has strong connection with the moon's phases, and the anchor cross gives us the assurance of weathering bad "storms"—and that's just to name a few!

What's nice about almost all cross motifs is the simplicity of design. Nearly anyone can draw them with little trouble.

Crystals *see* **Stones**

Cup Anything with a shape similar to a cup represents the feminine aspect, water, receptivity, and the lunar nature. The circle of the labyrinth, maze, and mandala is an overturned cup, completely poured out!

Cylinders Cylinders with seals upon them, or those bearing special herbs and stones within, were often used by the ancients as amulets and charms. In the case of the former, the magick was released when the seal was imprinted in wax. The latter filled cylinders allowed people to carry magick with them no matter where they were. This second option is certainly functional in sacred pattern work. Find a test tube or small bottle that you can fill with symbolic plant matter, oils, stones, or whatever and carry it in your labyrinth-walking activities. Also carry it afterward to keep the magick moving!

Daath The abyss in Kabbalism, which is an inbetween place where form exists without substance—effectively the realm in which magickal potential abides before we do something to bring it forth.

Divine names In Islamic tradition there are 99 excellent names for god and the person who can recite them shall enter Paradise. Now, I don't expect anyone to go out and memorize these names, but they might be something you could use in word labyrinths or mandalas as borders to guide your path. Here is a sampling of those names:

- Al-Basir: meaning seer (good for motivating insight)
- Al-Chaffar: meaning forgiver (good for inspiring self-forgiveness too)
- Al-Fattah: meaning opener (good for creating or recognizing opportunities)
- Al-Hadi: meaning guide (good for intuitive/spontaneous efforts)
- Al-Hakk: meaning truth (good for stimulating honesty with self, others, and the divine)
- Al-Muhaimin: meaning protector (good for all patterns)
- Al-Muhyi: meaning quickener (good for maze work or when you need fast manifestation)
- Ar-Rahim: meaning compassionate (good choice for mandalas)

As an aside, there's nothing that says you have to rely only on this list. The world's religious traditions have given thousands of names to the Sacred Parent, and it was quite common to find those names written or spoken in conjunction with magickal rites. Use those names with which you have a strong affinity or those that best represent your goal.

Dog The image of a dog, or paw prints, are often a sign of assistance and help, usually that given by a trusted friend. In spontaneous exercises, this may indicate a need to reach out and ask for that help rather than trying to remain the proverbial island. In planned patterns, use the dog to inspire devotion, loyalty, or motivate the spirit of cooperation.

Dolphin A very popular creature in New Age circles, dolphin images connect us with the breath of life, and our ability to move between two worlds—flesh and spirit (mandala).

Dove The dove pattern appears in many stained glass window designs, flying down toward believers with a message of purity and peace. This bird reminds us that maintaining good spiritual hygiene and harmony between people are among our two greatest duties as metaphysical seekers.

Dragonfly Good luck; regeneration; rapid changes

Eight The number eight is a stabilizing force, being twice the power of four. It represents harmony, transformation, and a person's inner life.

When turned on its side, the eight becomes an infinity sign, pointing toward the soul's eternal nature and the limitless potential of humankind. Eight's power color is black.

Elephant The elephant is a symbol of moderation and wisdom. It is also the trusted bearer of tradition and history. Use an elephant in your patterns when you're trying to reconnect with your "roots" or develop restraint.

Eleven Eleven is the number of conflict and challenges. It most often appears in spontaneous patterns where someone is facing controversy or strife, or feels as if they're facing a brick wall.

Equal sign While this can obviously mean agreement and conformity, it can also represent a wider path, parallels, and symmetry. Where does this pattern go to in your labyrinth? Does it end at another emblem? Are you walking in the middle of the lines to maintain balance, or breaking out of them to experience liberation? These are the questions and lessons in this symbol.

Eye In Egypt a stylized eye represents the great god Ra, watching over the Egyptian people. Over the aeons, this symbol and other versions of it have come to symbolize divinely inspired understanding, vision (both physical and spiritual), and esoteric mysteries that we are still seeking to comprehend.

In spontaneous patterns the image of an eye can indicate a sense of misgiving, as if you're being watched. Alternatively, in conjunction with other emblems or at the center of a mandala, it illustrates having your eye on something (often a goal).

Eye of Horus This appears on the Great Seal of the U.S. as representing watchfulness and vigil. It is a perfect mandala in and of itself, which you could color and carry to remain attentive, or as part of a maze activity to heighten mental keenness.

Fate Three triangles that join at the point creates the Greek emblem of fate, which was also known to the Teutons and Romans. A good symbol to consider when you're focusing on future paths and decisions.

The alternative way of depicting fate is by using three intersecting circles, which also has some connections with love and marriage rituals (this is how we come by passing wedding cake through a ring three times).

Feather Intimately connected with the symbolic value of birds, feathers can also be pattern pointers. Turn the tip of a feather where you wish the energy to go! Make a feather flower for blossoming spirituality, or superimpose the image of a feather over a portrait of your burdens to help lighten the load.

Since feathers were once used as pens, they make an excellent emblem for focusing on your words. In this case, make the quill end of the feather ink-colored and then put this in the middle of your labyrinth pattern.

Fifty A number denoting joy and celebration. It marks a new cycle after seven, seven-year cycles.

Fish A very well-known Christian symbol for miracles, a simple fish design can also represent profuseness and/or the water element in your labyrinth-walking activities. Additionally, the simplest fish motif made from two curved lines facing each other and crossing at one end can symbolize the ancient goddess in her maiden and crone aspect (the waxing and waning moon).

Alternatively in Finnish lore fairies hate the smell of fish, so this might be a good central point in a devic protective mandala. Finally, for those who wish to conceive, the fish is an ancient helper of women who provides fertility.

Five The number of physicality (five fingers; five senses), organic awareness, self truths, and quintessential nature. In

Islamic tradition, five equates to prayer so it might be a good number of turns or segments in labyrinth work aimed at developing your communications with the Sacred. Also, in esoteric traditions five is the perfect number to use in spells or other procedures aimed at safeguarding yourself from the "evil eye," which in today's vernacular equates to negative vibes.

Flower Nature's mandala that represents the soul opening and accepting the light of spirit into itself for growth and awareness. A lot of flower motifs show up in mandalas and labyrinths, the most popular of which was the rose. More specific interpretive value or magickal energies for your efforts will depend on the type of flower you choose and how you integrate it (as an aromatic, carrying it, drawing it, etc.).

Consider getting yourself a book that includes the metaphysical correspondences of flowers like *The Herbal Arts* to use as a reference in making this decision. Here's a brief sampling to get you started:

- Anemone: transformation; wind magick
- Carnation: honor; promises
- Chrysanthemum: knowledge; long life; family
- Dandelion: fertility; divinatory ability
- Honeysuckle: a generous heart
- Iris: Hope; rising over circumstance; valor; faith
- Jasmine: love; beauty; spiritual contentment
- Lily: purity; peace; often attributed to the goddess
- Lotus: perfection; creation; purity; cycles
- Magnolia: prosperity; favors; heroic energy
- Marigold: prophesy; psychic abilities
- Orchid: perfection
- Pansy: thoughtfulness; remembrance; love
- Peony: wealth and good fortune; fertility; anti-magick
- Sunflower: solar and fire-related magick
- Violet: humility; love; wishes

Special note to cooks: Many flowers are edible! They make an excellent source of vitamins for vegetarians, and a whimsical addition to your magickal menus.

Footprints or shoe prints Symbolic of the path you have already walked, or those who have taken this road before you. Each step taken keeps the magick moving!

Forty The number of completion and wholeness; also the traditional time of hermitage. (Moses spent forty days in the wilderness to receive the Commandments, for example.)

Four The number four symbolizes our limits. It is the rational mind, life's patterned rhythms, harmonic order, and the number of earth itself. By using this number in labyrinth walking you can rediscover the interrelatedness of all earth's creatures (including people). You can also reestablish or create new foundations for yourself, and give your dreams a secure place in which to grow. Four's energy can be improved by using it in predominantly brown, green, or other earth-toned mazes to emphasize the conscious self.

Frog Among shamans the frog represents healing. In other settings it symbolizes fertility. In either case, this might give rise to an elaborate game of leap frog in wellness mandala activities, or the idea of carrying a frog image when walking a labyrinth to inspire fruitfulness.

Fruit Fruit-shaped patterns aren't overly difficult to draw into your labyrinth-walking activities. Alternatively you can use the essential oils of fruits as an aromatic cue, or eat them before an effort to help internalize specific types of energy patterns. Here's a brief list of the symbolic value in common fruits:

- Apple: health; knowledge; redemption; love
- Apricot: faithfulness; aphrodisiac qualities
- Cherry: what you must give up or release to receive
- Date: vitality; abundance; male virility
- Fig: fertility; enlightenment
- Grape: peace; plenty; celebration

- Lemon: anti-magick charm; love
- Lime: improved communication between lovers (the Virgin Dance maze)
- Orange: good luck; dedication; prosperity
- Peach: long life; wisdom; beauty
- Pineapple: hospitality; well-being
- Plum: fertility; fidelity
- Pomegranate: sun magick; feminine fertility
- Strawberry: love; health; fruitfulness

Gateway In Shinto tradition the outside supports of a gate are designed to reach to heaven. And, of course, the gate stands outside the temple marking the entry to a sacred space. In large efforts gates could be used similarly. Otherwise, the symbolic value of a gate in a maze or mandala might be as a way to change your direction or move past a particularly difficult point in your life.

Gebhurah The fifth circuit in the Kabbalistic tree of life representing time and motion, and our ability to recognize "reality" in terms of both these factors. In some translations the word Pahad appears, meaning justice.

Globe A three-dimensional circle, this makes a good prop for labyrinths and mazes, and if you want to cover one with paper it could become a 3-D mandala. The globe represents similarly global thinking and a mentality that dares to go beyond the linear self like Daedelus did.

Gold Gold has very strong ties with yellow but on a higher vibrational level. This is the color of the sun, a traditional hue for royalty, and the pigment chosen to represent the masculine aspect of the divine. Consequently, adding gold to mazes is a great idea since it works cooperatively with the rational, logical self. In mandalas and labyrinths gold is suited to stressing physical energy or wellness, and your ability to take authority in a situation.

God and Goddess symbols Each culture has unique symbols for the god and goddess, and even those may vary depending on the facet of the divine about whom they're talking. However, in modern times I think we have a simple alternative open to us—the emblems used to mark the men's and women's rooms in public places! These are simple to draw, and perfect generic representations of the male/female aspects.

Green Nature's key color, green bears the energy of rebirth, growth, tangible progress, true natural beauty, elemental forces, and taking care of business literally or figuratively. It is also the color associated with the heart chakra, meaning green is an excellent choice to include when designing mandalas for emotional healing. In labyrinths, add green to your borders when you want to surround yourself and your efforts with protection from the elemental forces, and/or positive energy for advancement. Any green-themed labyrinth-walking activity will be augmented by working on a Wednesday or when the moon is in Cancer.

Hammer Having been an attribute of several blacksmith gods, a hammer represents the tempering of our spirits. Because of its use as a modern tool it can also represent "hammering home" the point of the mandala.

Hand The symbol of assistance; a ready tool at your disposal that comes from the self. The Egyptians used the image of an open hand to represent generosity. For labyrinth walking this might equate to learning how to give and receive with equal grace.

In spontaneous pattern making, pay particular attention to where the hand points, how many fingers are showing (numeric value), and what (if anything) the hand holds. This additional information will provide you with more insights.

In planned activities, use a hand pattern as a five-course labyrinth to emphasize being true to yourself, as the center of a mandala to make you more aware and appreciative of your skills or your blessings, and as part of mazes where you want to stress the thought–action connection.

Heart The emotional nature. Bear in mind that our emotions have a lot of different dimensions. For example, there is the love of self, others, children, pets, a job, an art, money, or whatever. So something lying within or near the heart, or its color, can be particularly meaningful.

Henna This plant was known to the Egyptians and was used as a red dye for women's mysteries. By washing your hands and feet in this before working a labyrinth, you connect with the ancient goddess. Because this leaves a temporary "tatoo" you can also use henna to draw your patterns upon yourself so that the magick unfolds in and with you. By the way, the art of henna tattooing is called Mehndi.

Herbs Herbs can be used in grown patterns, as aromatics for your labyrinth-walking activities, or their shapes added to a specific design according to the symbolic value of the herb. Here are just a few (I've limited this list to common culinary herbs):

- Basil: healing ire; physical vitality
- Bay leaves: love; devotion; success
- Cinnamon: energy; passion; longevity
- Clove: peace; banishing gossip; inspiring romance
- Dill: protection (against witchcraft); restful sleep
- Garlic: safety; cleansing
- Ginger: energy; the fire element
- Marjoram: happiness; mental keenness (good for mazes); settling a restless spirit (a mandala pattern)
- Mint: hospitality; virtue; health
- Nutmeg: psychism and vision
- Rosemary: improving memory; fidelity
- Sage: health and wisdom
- Thyme: bravery; communing with fairy folk; positive dreams

Hexagrams The best known of these images is the Star of David (protection), but hexagrams were popular in many settings for magick. In India, for example, they were used to represent the connection between Kali and Shiva which maintains ongoing energy in the universe (mandala).

Rather than a traditional hexagram, magicians sometimes used one where the center point interlaced, more than likely to bind energy therein. This also neatly allowed the whole pattern to be created from an unbroken line, which provided more protective energy and flowing energy.

It's easier to use hexagrams for your labyrinth-walking efforts if, after you make them, you erase the lines that cross over other lines—this gives you a built-in path!

Hod The number eight in the Kabbalistic tree of life, representing thoughtfulness. Some people alternatively interpret this point as symbolizing prominence.

Hogan This dwelling construction traditional to the Navajos is representative of the cosmos, with the doorway facing east to greet the sun. This pattern, in two dimensional form, would make a lovely starting point for a mandala or outer perimeter for a labyrinth. Additionally, since the door faces east (the center of consciousness) it could be used in maze work too.

Horse Channeling your instincts in a positive manner. A good alternative to drawing a horse is simply using a horseshoe, which also stresses good luck and the lunar nature.

Hourglass Time's natural movement. What must transpire before manifestation happens.

IAW or **IAO** These three letters come from an old Gnostic amulet. They are said to represent not only the name of God, but the second version can also mean "the existing." Consequently this would make a good word to place at the center of an "I am" mandala.

Kether The number one in the Kabbalistic tree of life, representing the point of the mandala—an idea that has not quite yet found definition but whose total potential already exists. It is also the link between wisdom and understanding.

Key In many traditions the gatekeepers of heaven, and those who oversee the mysteries, bear keys (either physical or verbal). With this in mind, the key bears the symbolic value of openings and closings, along with wisdom, maturity, and success. It can also represent protecting those things that you hold dear. All in all, a good charm to carry in maze work.

Knife or **sword** As one of the sacred tools of Wicca, an athame might make an excellent choice of implements to etch out the pattern of your labyrinth-walking effort. It has long been used as part of drawing the sacred space in magickal traditions, so the symbolism is doubly apt.

Knives and swords can also be depicted in any of the patterns or carried with you on labyrinth-walking activities to represent several things. First, if the knife/sword has two edges it symbolizes the duality of self—good and bad. Second, it can symbolize a cutting away or separation.

Knot Leonardo da Vinci created a contemplative labyrinth diagram from one long thread that, after many knots, led to the center of self. The knot binds energy in place, or can release it depending on how you use it.

Labrys Discussed briefly in the chapter on labyrinths, this can represent amazonlike female power, or the cutting fierceness of certain god figures like Thor, Ptah, and the Mayan god known simply as "god of the Axe." The name *labyrinth* may have developed from this ancient emblem since in Crete the pattern was called "house of the double axe."

Ladder or **stairs** In Egypt the steps amulet (which looks like a series of five stairs) represents that which separates the lower and upper worlds. For our purposes this translates as ascension, a pathway between earth and heaven, or rising above our circumstances.

Lamp (oil style) Good luck, wish magick, wisdom, elemental powers like the gini. A lightbulb may be a substitute here, and represents ideas and inspiration. See also **Candle**.

Leaf Leaf motifs are very suited to mazes (a choice of paths) and to mandalas because of their symmetrical nature. In mazes specifically, the leaf pattern represents equally appealing options. Even so, leaves will generally have one main branch. It will be up to you to decide if you want to use that vein for nourishment or find another way, so consider this pattern for decision-making labyrinths too.

As an interesting aside, studies have shown that the pattern of a leaf visually follows the tree from which it comes. So, an alternative interpretation in spontaneous activities might be a need to return to your source, your roots, for greater understanding.

Lightning Dynamic energy that can either fertilize or destroy. When lightning extends from the center of a pattern beyond its border, this often indicates explosive anger directed at a person or situation. When it moves in from outside the pattern, you may be feeling as if unwarranted wrath is being directed toward you. When lightning is sealed within the pattern, consider if you've been angry toward yourself lately.

When this kind of energy is recognized and channeled effectively, it can be very helpful (the objective example here being electricity). So you can certainly use lightning's symbolic nature in a planned pattern to empower your effort. One example I saw of this was a mandala in which eight lightning bolts radiated from the center as a way of encouraging a well-controlled, but forceful transformation.

Life tree This oriental motif, consisting of one vertical line crossed by four equidistant horizontal lines, represents the soul's journey as a pilgrimage where the ultimate goal is to become one's priest or priestess, purify the spirit, and attain enlightenment. It is perfectly suited to all three sacred patterns we've discussed in this book, but perhaps uniquely so to a maze because of the options presented, and the decisions necessary to obtaining this goal.

Line The path, self, or singularity. The direction of the line and/or its angle can have significance too. For example, straight lines are considered masculine, while curved lines are feminine. If you draw a spontaneous mandala that has a lot of left-tilted lines, it might indicate an over-emphasis on left-brain thinking, a tendency toward negativity, or some other type of influence that's got you off center.

Lion Traditionally an image of strength and a fighting spirit. A good symbol to choose when you need to build courage or stand your ground (a lion's paw design is a perfectly good alternative here).

Malkuth The number ten in the Kabbalistic tree of life representing the fully manifested person who has gone through the first nine levels of awareness to achieve the "kingdom" of enlightenment. This is also the point at which someone truly takes the reins of control back and becomes a co-creator with the divine.

Mask Add a mask to your labyrinth-walking activities to challenge self-images that were culturally or environmentally conceived. Alternatively use this tool as a way of connecting with specific spiritual forces (like devas or animal guides).

Mathematical symbols One should never overlook the newer symbols that have become a part of our everyday life, and mathematical representations certainly qualify. For example:

+ : (addition): to grow in size or quality
− : (subtract): to lessen or decline
÷ : to separate
= : equality and balance; balancing the equation of life
× : multiply energy
% : giving only a certain portion; an allotment

Minerals and **Metals** Like stones and crystals noted later in this section, metals and minerals can be integrated into your labyrinth-walking activities by carrying them as charms and amulets, by burying them in the ground near where you're working, by patterning them into small rock gardens, or placing them on the altar in specially configured designs. Here's some metal and mineral correspondences for your consideration:

Brass: healing; prosperity

Copper: luck; money; love

Gold: the god aspect (maze); success and victory

Iron: protection (spiral maze); vitality; grounding

Lead: divination; foundations; safety

Loadstone: attracting love, truth, and virility

Pyrite: prosperity and good fortune (mandala)

Salt: protection and purification. Consider using this to
    mark the periphery of your labyrinth-walking efforts

Silver: lunar energy (labyrinth); dreams and psychic
    awareness

Tin: luck, especially with money

Mirror or **Mirrored surface** A very powerful symbol. It accents
the role you play as a co-creator in your personal destiny and
also indicates that the answers you need are truly within. Perhaps that's why in Egyptian the words for mirror and life are
the same!

A mirror is an excellent choice for the center of any sacred
patterns. In this position the mirror can also generate protective
energies, reflecting away any negatives. Beyond this, because
of its connections with scrying it might be something to carry or
add to patterned work aimed at improving divinatory insight.

Mouse Mice generally have correlations with prudence or the
ability to slip into and out of places without being seen. This
might relate well to the maze, especially since mice have been
used by science in this setting.

For those of you who can't find a mouse image or can't
draw one, don't overlook the mouse that's in most houses
these days—the one at your computer!

Musical Note Finding your keynote—the music in your soul,
or your healing song (in shamanism).

Nandyavarta A Hindu design, this is a perfect labyrinth unto
itself. There are, however, three choices of routes to the center

which represents the subconscious, intuitive self. Very effective as it stands.

Nefer Nefer means graciousness or pleasantness. An Egyptian symbol that was often made into amulets to confer youth, joy, strength, and luck. This looks like an oval with a line extending upward from the top-center. This line is crossed by two others at the tip, the first being longer than the second at the tip. What's interesting here is that if done in sand or cloth this can create various "hallways" from which to choose—an interesting motif for maze work.

Net An ingathering (e.g., casting one's net upon the spiritual waters and gathering what awaits you there).

Netzach or **Nesakh** The number seven in the Kabbalistic tree of life, this figure represents success and victory, of recognizing a certain quality of existence and finding peace in it.

Nine This is the number of beneficent spiritual beings like angels and guides. As 3×3 it is also a number that signifies the manifestation of spiritual or magickal power. When nines start showing up a lot in your spontaneous activities, be forewarned that your metaphysical self is trying to break through. You may start having psychic experiences or notice dramatic changes in the way you practice your magickal arts. Similarly, when you want these type of changes, plan your patterns with nine turns or segments.

Numbers Numbers from 1–10, 12, 40, 50, and 60 are covered separately in this section. In considering numbers, don't forget that they can be represented by Roman numerals, Hebrew characters, Devanagari (Arabic numerals), and by the segments in your mandala, by the paths in the maze, or the circuits in the labyrinth.

Obelisk This word translates from the Greek meaning pointed pillar. Consequently it's very suited to the "point" of the mandala, or in 2-D form as a pointer in your labyrinth-walking efforts.

One The number one represents the monad of identity and the god/self. In spontaneous efforts it may reveal the feeling that you are alone, or that you need to make yourself a priority. It also represents human potential, and a beginning, in that it's where we start counting sequences.

Use singular colors or patterns when you need to focus on wholeness within. Or, use one predominant pattern in mandalas to make the energy of that pattern the "point" or to stress unity in what that pattern represents.

Owl Knowledge and wisdom of the ages, and the human quest to understand our place in the greater scheme of things. In Native American tradition an owl's feather symbolizes the need to be real, to truly know and accept the self. It is for this reason that owls pose the question, "Who are you?"

Use owl symbolism in your patterned work when your quest is one of self-awareness without judgement.

Peace sign While a more modern pictograph, the peace sign is something that has immediate meaning and an impact on our awareness. Since it's encompassed by a circle, and the Y is symmetrically centered, this is a natural mandala perfect for generating harmony (the Y strongly resembling the protective rune too). The branching pathway could also be used in maze activities to denote the conscious choice to live in peace with self and others.

Pen or **quill** The responsibility for our words; effective communication.

Pictographic writing The people of Egypt, Summeria, Babylon, Cameroon, China, Japan, and even among Mayan and Cherokee cultures all had unique pictographic writing systems where a picture was, indeed, worth a thousand words! While each of these languages could not be covered in this dictionary, they are well worth looking into for alternatives or additions to your pattern work. Look specifically to Hieroglyph, Cuneiform writing, Cartouche, and Calligraphy for more ideas.

Pillars Singularly a symbol of resilience and support. In groups of three it represents beauty, strength, and wisdom, as in Solomon's temple.

Planetary emblems The ancients believed that the planets were really wandering spirits whose energies affected life below. They also ascribed significance to each of the planets' energies. This means that the symbols associated with the planets can be placed in your patterns to build and emphasize the effect you're creating. Here's a brief list of the planetary symbol correspondences:

Sun: masculine powers; the light of consciousness (particularly good choice for maze work)
Moon: feminine powers; the subconscious and intuitive self (labyrinth oriented)
Venus: matters of love and luxury
Mercury: matters requiring communication, movement, and manifestation (mandala oriented)
Mars: matters requiring courage and strength, especially in the face of opposition
Jupiter: matters of leadership and authority; search for knowledge (maze oriented)
Saturn: matters of time and discipline, orderliness and responsibility (maze oriented)
Neptune: inspiration and idealism; dreams and fantasy
Uranus: surprises and inventiveness; dramatic change
Pluto: major changes and personal power; hidden forces

Poppet Small stuffed dolls often used for healing, love, and other types of sympathetic magick; at first this might not seem overly useful to labyrinth walking. Consider making a sacred pattern and a poppet that represents you, then moving the doll through the pattern. From a magickal perspective a symbol is just as powerful as what it represents, so you can spiritually move through the maze, mandala, or labyrinth you've created to collect the energy via your poppet!

Prohibition sign This red circle with a slash through it is easily recognized as saying *NO,* do not proceed. Good for banishing activities.

Purple The traditional color of royalty, purple represents leadership, divine callings, generosity, positive change (especially personal growth), and the Hermit card of the Tarot (the need to separate oneself temporarily in order to reunite harmoniously).

The lavender hue of purple represents the mystical nature, balanced by pink which is physical. The Crown chakra is purple to remind us of our link to the heavens. Purple's energy can be augmented by patterns that have three segments or courses, by working on a Thursday, or timing your effort for when the moon is in Virgo, Sagittarius, or Gemini.

Rainbow Uplifting hope. In spontaneous workings this represents something in yourself or a situation that brings encouragement. It is a benevolent sign that can be an alternative bridge symbol—marking a way across the impossible cavern (often of a more spiritual nature). Alternatively, it can symbolize a mystery being resolved through unordinary means (like magick).

Rainbows work fairly well in labyrinths as consecutive courses that take you progressively through the chakras. They also often appear in mandalas as the point for bringing hope to your heart, or as the border to keep heartening energies around you.

Recycle Another emblem to come to us in modern times, the recycle symbol is an excellent mandala for earth awareness.

Red The color of life's blood, red has a very strong impact in labyrinth-walking activities. It represents vitality, action, acknowledgement, passion, justice, a zealous commitment to life, the ability to give and receive (sacrifice), and the element of fire. The Tibetans use red in mandalas to map the way for enlightenment (the outer ring is often red), and alchemists considered it a symbol of progress. Red is the spin of magick (the base chakra), and its energy can be increased by placing it in patterns with nine courses or segments, by working on a Tuesday, or timing your effort for when the moon is in Aries or Scorpio.

Runes By best estimates, runes have been used as a symbolic language for over two thousand years. This gives them a lot of potential in your labyrinth-walking activities. Use them as part of the layout, put one at a specific juncture to mark a change in energy, make one the center point of a maze, etc. Here's a list of the most commonly seen runes and their meanings:

Feoh, Fehu	prosperity; affluence and influence; success
Ur, Uruz	vitality, well being, fortitude
Thorn, Thurisaz	change and transformations
Os, Ansuz	counsel and communications; listen carefully
Rad, Raido	active energy; following through tenaciously
Ken, Kaunaz	comprehension; spiritual awakening
Gifu, Gebo	symmetry; benevolence; a boon granted
Win, Wunjo	joy; an uplifting opportunity
Haegel, Hagalaz	interruptions; stress
Nyo, Nauthiz	barriers to overcome; steadfastness
Iss, Issa	binding; standstill; hermitage
Ger, Jera	abundance; reward
Eoh, Eiwaz	strategy; order
Perth, Peord	possibilities; surprises
Eol, Algiz	protection
Sigil, Sowelu	inventiveness; victory; solar magick
Tir, Tiwaz	a sacred battle ends successfully
Beork, Berkana	development (positive); progress
Eh, Ehwaz	evolution that comes from effort
Man, Mannaz	modesty and self-awareness
Lager, Laguz	the unseen; flexibility
Ing, Inguz	right thought and action

Daeg, Dagaz   promise of improvements
Ethel, Othalaz   cultural or familial legacy/history

S Depending on what direction the S lays, it can have a variety of meanings. On its side it represents a winding path that will reach its goal, but not directly. In this position it can also symbolize the element of water (a wave), or being on a particular "wavelength."

Upright the S might portray a focus on financial matters (like an incomplete dollar sign). It may also represent what I call the "super-person" syndrome where someone is forever trying to be a hero. In spontaneous efforts a capital S often represents SELF.

Seasons The line drawings for the seasons can be used in various ways for your sacred patterns. In a mandala they might represent the four quarters. In the labyrinth, one of the seasons could be the "point" depending on its symbolic value for your goal. In the maze, a seasonal emblem might be an obstacle to overcome, or a distracting turn. Here's an overview of each season's energies:

Spring: a pattern that looks like sprouting vegetation, spring focuses on renewal and hope (mandala)
Summer: a pattern that looks like a matured sprout reaching to the sun, summer focuses on activity and socialization (labyrinth). Because the sun is so strong during this season, it's also a good time/pattern for maze work
Fall: a pattern that looks like a wilting plant, still routed in the earth, fall focuses on ingathering and saving our resources, both magickal and physical (inward turning labyrinth)
Winter: a pattern that looks like seeds hiding beneath the protective housing of earth, winter is a time of rest, meaning it might be best placed *outside* or at the completion of a pattern

Note that cultural variances on what patterns represent the seasons exist. These are just one example.

Scarab An Egyptian symbol for new life and new beginnings.

Scroll Basically an ancient book. In esoteric traditions scrolls symbolize time with the past at the beginning of the scroll and the future still unwound. Using this symbolism, you might want to try unrolling a small scroll of paper, like Ariadne's Thread, during a labyrinth walk. At the end of the scroll write the amount of time in which you want the magick to manifest.

Serpent, Double-headed A water symbol, representing fertilizing rain that could be applied in a figurative sense to refresh our spirits and our creative nature.

Seven Seven is the number of orientation, of getting our bearings. It also represents time (the days of the week), and is often considered lucky when it appears in random divination systems. Cultures as diverse as the Celts and Assyrians felt this number had mystical powers, specifically for harmony, synchronicity, and spiritual awareness. So when it appears in spontaneous efforts, consider it a good sign!

Shell A lot here depends on what type of shell you choose to use. A scallop shell design is generally associated with feminine sexuality (like the goddess Venus), fortune in love, and passion. The conch shell is associated with announcements and the sense of hearing, and cowrie shells symbolize the ability to foresee the future and discern patterns in the present.

Shen An Egyptian pictograph of a circle sitting on a line (somewhat like a sun setting on the line of the horizon). This symbol represents the power of the sun god, and eternity. It might be suited to the exterior of a maze considering the solar/masculine connection.

Shield Shields have totemic energy for protection, courage, speed, and agility. Some people like to make mandala-styled shields or medicine shields that represent a Path, a goal, or elemental powers safeguarding a sacred space.

Silver The color of the moon which represents the feminine, intuitive, sensitive self. Silver also has some heroic connotations having been the color of a knight's amour. When you need to figuratively "arm" yourself with the intuitive nature, make this a predominant color in your sacred patterns.

Six The number of creativity, fertility, fruitfulness, and evolution. Six stands on the edge of completion. The key here is to finish the cycle and therefore fulfill what you've started. In spontaneous patterns six can also represent overcoming an obstacle, often of a self-imposed nature. To understand the symbolic value further consider what creates the six—is it a color or objects? For example, a green six might reveal a jealous nature standing between you and a happy relationship. Or, six stars could indicate a fanciful person who needs to give their dreams foundations in which to manifest.

Sixty The Egyptian number of long life and time's passage.

Smile Seen often in the version of a happy face these days, the pictograph of a smile makes us think immediately of joy, so use it that way in your labyrinth-walking activities. Don't forget to get creative. For example, use the curve of a smile as part of your path in the labyrinth, or as part of the outer edge!

Snake This creature can be represented by the letter S, making it easy to integrate for your pattern work. Generally snakes represent life, longevity, health, and transformative ability (shedding skins in a metaphoric way).

Snowflake A lovely pattern for mandalas because of their symmetry, this represents individuality, truth, and wisdom.

Spider As one might expect the symbolism of the spider is connected to its web, representing destiny, the interconnectedness of all things (the mandala), and life's network. Because of various Native American myths, the spider can also represent our ability to communicate effectively.

Spear Spears have various symbolic values ascribed to them. For one, they often represent the god aspect, and so would be well suited to part of a maze's pattern. Second, they are often associated with fertility, being a type of phallic symbol.

Finally, if you lay the spear across your path it denotes a weakness or failing to be overcome, or a challenge to take up your spiritual weapons and fight the good fight.

Spiral The sacred spiral represents cycles. It also symbolizes the path to discovering vortices and the magickal cone of power that all witches use to direct spells and rituals. In Eastern traditions this image is equated with the chakras and kundalini energy. In Babylonia, spiral written incantations were used to trap malevolent spirits, giving rise to some ideas about using spiral labyrinths for trapping problems or sickness.

Note that spirals are in motion, either outward moving or inward moving. This is active energy, especially in terms of finding the point in your life's mandala. Think of this like spiritual DNA strands for creating a healthy, happy soul that rejoices in the individual and diversity.

Stones or **crystals** It's difficult to find large crystals that are reasonably priced these days, so I'd suggest using stones and crystals in labyrinth-walking activities as part of jewelry, as pocket amulets, as garden energy enhancers (buried in the dirt), as meditation points in the middle of a pattern, or as part of small patterned rock gardens. Here's a list of the symbolic value of common stones and crystals:

Agate (banded): protection and safety
Agate (black): courage and success
Agate (red): peace; protection from stormy situations
Amber: health and sun magick; self confidence (maze oriented)
Amethyst: harmony; personal control
Beryl: renewed hope; increasing psychism (mandala oriented)
Bloodstone: prosperity; business sense (maze oriented)
Carnelian: friendship; overcoming depression; communication
Cat's eye: perspective; longevity

Citrine: overcoming fears (labyrinth); increased awareness (mandala)

Coral: devotion and fidelity; health; wisdom

Fluorite: the conscious mind (maze)

Garnet: sincerity

Hematite: grounding and foundations; divinatory ability

Jade: love; accord

Jet: collects negativity

Lapis: happiness, self-love (mandala), devotion (labyrinth)

Moonstone: moon magick; luck (labyrinth oriented)

Onyx: banishing bad dreams

Quartz: energy; clarity (maze); healing (mandala)

Sodalite: peace; meditative skill (mandala); wisdom

Turquoise: safe travel; personal fulfillment

Square Temporal and earthly achievements. A definite place and time. Integrating lessons into one's daily reality. Also consider what's in or near the square as juxtaposed with our language. Is an item or person being "squared off" (observed and confronted), is it a truly "square deal" (meaning fair), is someone looking you "square in the eyes" (being honest), etc.

A double square (creating a star motif) is a symbol of the balance between order and chaos, making it uniquely suited to maze work.

Square/Circle, superimposed The microcosm vs. macrocosm or imperfect man versus perfection of the cosmos.

Star In planned activities these represent Universal patterns that offer guidance for our fulfillment, following after a dream and bringing it into manifestation, and/or our wishes. In spontaneous patterns stars can be positive and negative. For example, a star appearing in the center of an eye design could reveal a tendency to look at life through rose-colored glasses, or overestimate what you can do (being "starry eyed"). A star as the focal point of a mandala, however, might be a good sign that you're achieving your goals.

Star and **Crescent Moon** (combined) A traditional symbol of Islam, this represents devotion and faith.

Sword In the middle ages (and before) many Christian warriors used the hilt of a sword as a cross to which to direct their prayers, or to mark graves. With this in mind, the sword symbolizes heroic battles (but not always ones that are undertaken for the right reasons).

A two-edged sword symbolizes dichotomy and the dualistic nature of life and humankind (good/bad; light/dark). Depending on where a sword appears in your patterning activities it can also indicate a "cutting away" or perhaps an all-out battle to liberate yourself from something you fear or feel is unproductive.

Tassel Called a *Sisith* in Hebraic tradition, a tassel is worn on the edge of garments as amulets to drive away negativity and evil spirits. An alternative is blue fringe or a lock of hair attached to your clothing somewhere.

Tattvas In Hinduism these simple geometric figures represent the elements, and just drawing these patterns in the correct color invokes elemental powers. They are:

> Silver crescent moon: water
> Blue circle: air
> Red triangle: fire
> Yellow diamond: earth
> Black egg: akasa (spirit/ether)

Tau cross The Tau cross once represented the great oak tree and was a symbol that could bring fertilizing rain. Legend also claims that this is the symbol the Israelites painted on their doors at Passover. With this in mind, the Tau cross can be used at intersections of labyrinths and mazes, or as part of a mandala for strength (oak), fruitfulness (rain), and protection.

Teardrop Fertilizing rain, growth, cleansing, and healing. In spontaneous patterns pay particular attention to whether these are being held back or released by the border. This will tell you whether or not you've been honest with your emotions and letting them flow as needed to reclaim your wholeness.

Ten Ten is the number of morality, codes, and ethics. Use this in your patterns when you need to really focus on proper intention and motivation.

Textures One way of emphasizing your sense of touch is through textures, specifically in the clothing you choose to wear or by the fabric chosen for making large labyrinth-walking patterns. Here are some correspondences for specific textures:

- angora: comfort; tenderness
- chiffon: the air element; freedom
- corduroy: the channels of this fabric could be laid out following the circuits of a labyrinth to improve energy flow
- cotton: durability; simplicity
- denim: practicality; hard work
- fur: the tribal soul. Note that this can vary by type of animal, but in the interest of earth-friendliness I suggest fake fur instead
- lace: knot magick; love
- satin: formality; gracefulness
- silk: luxury; affluence
- wool (tartan): strong connection with Celtic/Scottish magick
- woven fabric: the weaving of fate or your magick

The way *you* respond to the textural quality of a material is more important than using this list verbatim.

Thorn In Shamanic beliefs nature often hides its greatest treasures behind specific obstacles like a thorn. So in your patterned motif, the thorn can represent a gift or prize that requires effort and tenacity to obtain.

Thread Very often associated with Fate and the story of Ariadne's assistance to Theseus. Try unraveling, collecting, or knotting thread of a sympathetic color (to release, gather, or bind/hold energy) as part of your labyrinth-walking efforts. Carry a snippet afterward as a charm or amulet to bear the magick with you.

Three The number three denotes vital energy in motion. There's also definition in this number: a beginning, middle, and end that intimates even more—rebirth. When three motifs or the number three shows up a lot in mandalas, consider what your dreams have been showing you, or what stories have had profound impacts on your life. Three's power color is purple or violet.

Tiphereth The number six in the Kabbalistic tree of life, this is a lovely term that means "beauty." Tiphereth is the point of self-actualization.

Torch Torches have analogous symbolism to candles as protective and illuminating in the spiritual sense. They're a nice touch to sundown stone or hedge maze-walking activities. And thanks to the Statue of Liberty, it might make an interesting addition to maze work—lighting the way for your mental growth.

Tortoise Use this pattern to emphasize determination, to manifest endurance for yourself or a project, or to increase your connection to the Ancestors.

Tree In nearly every culture the tree represents life. Its roots are your security and where it's founded. The bark represents personal fortitude and backbone. The branches indicate how far you're willing to reach out and up to touch others or achieve your goals.

If this is a spontaneously produced pattern, pay particular attention to each of the tree's parts. If you're uprooted, you don't have solid foundations and it's time to build them. If your bark is missing, you're overexposed. If your branches are very short and scraggly, you're holding back and being the proverbial wallflower.

Also, each tree has different symbolic value in nature's rich language. So if you're creating a hedge-style maze, mandala, or labyrinth you may wish to consider these correspondences:

- Ash: luck; longevity
- Beech: prosperity and divinatory ability
- Birch: birth or inception; fertility
- Cherry: the goddess; luck in love
- Elder: health; visions
- Hawthorn: magick; goddess energy
- Laurel: success; victory; purification
- Mulberry: the Chinese tree of life, this represents the three stages of life (youth, maturity, old age)
- Myrtle: good fortune, joy, and peace
- Oak: steadfastness; god-in-nature
- Pine: longevity, strength, and fertility
- Willow: grace in difficult situations; flexibility
- Yew: the immortal nature of the soul; anti-magick energy

Triangle In Indian the upward-pointing triangle is phallic, while a downward-pointing triangle represents the vulva, and the two together create an image of the ascending and descending centers of energy. Western psychology says the upward-pointing triangle represents creative energy, new projects, and assertiveness while the downward one may represent an ending and a delving into the subconscious on a more aware level (see also **Fate**).

Trigrams Taken from the divinatory system called the I-Ching (China), there are eight basic trigrams with specific meanings that might be applied to your labyrinth-walking efforts. Since each trigram is composed of three lines (whole or broken), they're very easy to draw:

Fire; sun; energy

Water (rain/stream); flow

Heaven; awareness; spirituality

Thunder; warnings; disruption

Hills/mountains; upward movement

Lakes; contained refreshment

Wind and wood; movement

Earth; foundations; temporal

Tryfus A rather unique pictograph that comes from the Isle of Man, this is a three-legged figure that appears to be running! Also called a Trip-pes, it represents the creative force of will. As such it would make a really neat outline for a labyrinthian-styled or maze effort.

Twelve Twelve is the number of cosmic order, heroism, and faith. It speaks strongly of a quest that's completed. It can also represent your ties to the Ancestors (of family or spirit). Twelve courses or segments in a labyrinth-walking activity is one good way to focus on the coming year or the cycles in your life.

Two Two major patterns in a labyrinth or the number two represents opposing forces—form versus function. Much here will depend on the rest of the imagery to know if those forces resolve themselves and achieve balance.

U A sudden turn about. Alternatively an opening through which one can get past the other restrictions around them. Upside down this emblem can represent a table over which something is discussed or let lie. Alternatively, in the runic alphabet the upside down U is called Uruz, and symbolizes personal change, strength, growth, and maturity.

Vegetables Some vegetables are fairly easy to draw into your labyrinth-walking patterns. Others, of a strong aromatic nature, can be used in incense or anointing oils. The rest might be best eaten before or after your effort to support the magick. Here's a list of some vegetable symbolism:

- Beans: the Ancestors; omens and signs; banishing; luck
- Cabbage: happy relationship; money
- Carrot: vision; love; passion
- Celery: prophetic abilities; insight
- Corn: providence; plenty; divinatory ability
- Cucumber: fertility (male); emotional equilibrium
- Eggplant: mischief; playfulness; love
- Mushroom: knowledge; enlightenment; fairy magick
- Olive: peace; reconciliation; success
- Onion: cosmic awareness; lunar magick; protection; love
- Pea: providence; marriage
- Potato: healing; sustenance
- Radish: protection; passion
- Tomato: love; good fortune
- Yam: plenty; foundations

Veil A piece of astral fabric is said to cover the space between the worlds. With this in mind, a veil can be hung at the entryway or just before the "point" of a labyrinth or maze to represent the line between world and not-world.

Web The network of life. Fate. Bringing forth an idea so it has presence and being. Communication skills. When a spontaneous pattern shows broken webs it often indicates a feeling of disconnectedness or a lack of willpower, without which magick cannot happen.

White Like black, white appears in many creation myths as pure, divine, creative light that gives life to the world and to human consciousness. White has a sacred quality and implies purity (think snow white), organization, synthesis, clear-mindedness followed by positive action, and general goodness. It is the color of enlightenment, which often requires some type of sacrifice to achieve.

Alchemically white is the color of psychological transformation. White's energies are augmented by working on a Monday (the moon's day) or by adding it to patterns bearing seven courses or segments.

Wolf A helper in finding your path, or the way to the point.

Words Words can fill in the point or edge of a mandala, create the boundary or rosette of the labyrinth, or become the key to a maze. Each language, of course, has its own pattern of power that can create tremendous magick when used wisely. (Only work in languages you understand or the outcome will suffer.) If you don't think this is true, just consider how our words harm or heal in everyday conversations. More information on word and name mandalas can be found in Chapter 2, then adapted to a maze or labyrinth motif.

Yellow A gentler version of gold, yellow symbolizes friendly communications, kindness, continuity, charm, child-like joy, self-actualization, optimism, and faith. It corresponds to the solar plexus chakra, and can be augmented by timing your effort for when the moon is in Libra or Taurus. In China yellow paper is preferred for written or hand-drawn charms, so it might be worth considering for similar applications in your labyrinth activities. It is also a good color to consider in patterns designed to prepare you for new learning experiences.

Yesod The number nine in the Kabbalistic tree of life, this sigil represents the sense of foundation, being, and realness that we develop with maturity.

Ziggurat The Mesopotamian version of a step-style pyramid, the top was the meeting place between mortals and the divine. As such, if you lay the Ziggurat flat (2-D), put four of them with the tops meeting together (looks somewhat like a

Cross Patee), and enclose this image in a circle; it would make a lovely mandala for communing with the divine.

Zodiac signs As with the planets, you can place one (or a combination of) sign(s) of the zodiac into your sacred patterns to create a variety of energies that support your goals. Here is an overview of what each sign's emblem evokes:

Aries: energy, creativity, enthusiasm, and new beginnings

Taurus: stability, practicality, reliability, and tenacity

Gemini: the mental plane (good for mazes); humor

Cancer: lunar energies (good for labyrinths); focus on family

Leo: dynamic personality, generosity, courage, and finding one's "voice"

Virgo: analytical skill, caution, and good judgement (good for mazes)

Libra: balance, justice, fairness, and harmony (good for mandalas)

Scorpio: end of something old but the beginning of psychic awakening; passion; privacy

Sagittarius: introspection and perspective (good for mandalas); gypsy nature

Capricorn: making the best out of bad situations

Aquarius: social consciousness; personal independence; higher ideals (mandala energy)

Pisces: psychism, creativity, changability, and soul-searching (labyrinth oriented)

Gods and Goddesses of Mazes, Labyrinths, Mandalas and Patterns

Expatiate free o'er all this scene of man, A mighty maze,
but not without a Plan

—Alexander Pope, *Essay on Man*

Throughout the world's history humankind has often turned to a facet of the Divine for help with daily life and magickal arts. Many individuals today choose to do likewise. If you are among this group, I see no reason not to call upon your personal vision of the god/dess to aid, bless, and empower your labyrinth-walking activities. If you do not have a specific divine visage in mind, these resources will help.

Here I've assembled a sampling of but a few global gods and goddesses whose attributes can help you with sacred pattern creation. For mazes, I've included some deities who preside over the rational mind. For labyrinths I've included some deities who preside over the intuitive self, and similarly for mandalas I've included a few deities who assist in reclaiming our personal sanctity and wholeness.

If you decide to invoke or invite any of these Beings into your sacred space, please do so with respectfulness. Prepare your labyrinth-walking activity so it honors this persona (perhaps use some of the offerings/decorations suggested in this list). Also research more about that god's or goddess' personality and the culture in which they were represented. Learn how to say His or Her name correctly! These gestures mean a lot and will lead to more successful communions.

Adibuddha (Hindu) The ultimate male essence in Hindu Buddhism, this god's energy is suited to maze work, or the point of the mandala as representing enlightenment. Honor him with lotus.

Aditi (Hindu) Mother goddess who birthed the twelve gods of the months and who presides over matters of protection and guidance. Suited to twelve point/segment motifs. Honor her by working on Sunday.

Aengus MacOg (Irish) A youthful god suited to love mazes and labyrinths. Anything that uplifts the emotion of love is sacred to him.

Aeons (Gnostic) Goddesses of power and manifested thought (the point of the mandala or the path out of the labyrinth). Honor them by using the number eight or twenty-two in your pattern somehow.

Agassou (Benin/Haitian) Guardian god of custom and tradition, this deity represents the path of the labyrinth or maze. Honor him with spring water.

Ahsonnutli (Navajo) Hermaphroditic deity and creator, this god represents the point of the mandala.

Ahura Mazda (Persian) Lord of knowledge who presides over matters of goodness and who gave birth to universal laws (mandala energy). Honor him with kind acts and feathers.

Aker (Egyptian) This god watches over the meeting point of the east and west (mandala) as a gatekeeper. He is also a solar god (maze) who may be honored with lion images or gold hues.

Amun Ra (Egyptian) God of the sun (maze) who can be honored with turquoise, olive oil, or cedar incense.

Anagke (Greek) Goddess of necessity (maze) and destiny (labyrinth and mandala).

Anna Perenna (Roman) Goddess of the succession of years and cycles (labyrinth and mandala). Honor her with barley or twelve-pointed motifs.

Anu (Assyro-Babylonian) God of destiny (Ariadne's Thread). Honor him with any woven item or star motifs.

Apis (Egyptian) The sacred bull of Egypt (the minotaur), and an incarnation of Osiris. Honor him with willow, quartz, or ivy.

Apollo (Greek/Roman) God of creativity, health, and eloquence (mandala oriented), honor him with bay leaves, sunflower, cinnamon, or orchids.

Arachne (Greek) Spider goddess whose web can become Ariadne's Thread or the pattern of the mandala. Honor her with spider images.

Ashnan (Sumerian) Grain goddess suited to maize mazes. Honor her with cultivated items.

Athena (Greek) Goddess of intelligence (maze), arts, and peace (mandala). Honor her with flute music or geraniums.

Attis (Anatolian) A resurrected god of cycles and restoration (mandala), honor him with snowdrops, lamps, and bread.

Aya (Assyro-Babylonian) Goddess of law, order (maze), and justice (mandala). Honor her with solar imagery.

Bacabs (Mayan) The god of the four corners of creation (mandala), this is also a suitable god for any square motif maze or labyrinth. Honor him with rain water.

Baduh (Semitic) God of messages and understanding (maze), invoke him by writing the numbers eight, six, four, two or by designing your maze with those numbers integrated into it.

Baldur (Scandinavian) Sun god who is associated with wisdom (mandala or maze).

Bast (Egyptian) Goddess of playfulness (maze) and dance (labyrinth). Honor her with cat images.

Befana (Italian) Goddess of magick and gift-bearer (mandala or labyrinth). Honor her by sweeping the sacred space with a broom.

Benten (Japanese) Goddess of love (mandala), communication, music, luck, money, and patron of game players (maze). Honor her with dragon images, swords, or ships.

Benzaiten (Japanese) Goddess of the arts who can inspire your creativity for pattern creation. Honor her with anything you've made by hand.

Bes (Egyptian) A god of merry-making and playfulness, suited to maze work. Honor him with lively music.

Biame (Aborigine) A god of mischief whose energies suit the maze. Honor him with lunar items.

Blodeuwedd (Welsh) Goddess whose face is formed from oak, broom, and meadowsweet who also helps us break out of old cycles and outmoded ideas (labyrinth and mandala, or hedge mazes). Honor her with any of the three plants mentioned or owl imagery.

Brighid (Irish) Goddess of fertility and inspiration (mandala). Honor her with lit candles, images of arrows, or by working on February 1.

Brihaspati (Hindu) A teacher to the gods whose wisdom can help in either maze or mandala work. Honor him with the written sign for, or an image of, the planet Jupiter.

Buddha (Indian) The enlightened one who achieved oneness with the point of the mandala. Particularly helpful with eight-pointed motifs to represent the eightfold path. Honor him with topaz or lotus.

Buddhi (Tibetan) Goddess of intelligence (maze) and intuition (labyrinth). Honor her with elephant imagery.

Bunjil (Australia—Kulin) God of breath suited to mantra work for any sacred patterns. Honor him with rainbows or wind.

Byelbog (Slavonic) Protector of the forests. Call on him in hedge mazes and labyrinths, or when making floral mandalas. Honor him with fresh greenery.

Carmenta (Roman) Goddess who invented the Roman alphabet (written patterns), and who also presides over prophesy (mandala). Honor her with any art or by writing your pattern without vowels (which she keeps for herself).

Cerridwen (Welsh) Grain goddess (maize mazes), and guardian of the elixir that bestows inspiration (mandala) and knowledge (maze). Honor her with cauldrons or corn.

Chia (Columbian) Moon goddess (labyrinth) whose mischievous nature also makes her a good helper for maze work. Honor her with silver or other lunar items.

Chimaera (Greek) A goddess whose name has come to mean "illusion," making this a suitable figure to help with maze work. Honor her with oat or lion imagery.

Chukem (Columbia) God of foot races who can help you with maze work.

Coyote (Native American) A trickster spirit who, if properly appeased, may help you unlock the secrets of the maze.

Dakinis (Tibetan) Goddesses who rule over psychic energy (labyrinth/mandala). Honor them with anything beautiful or graceful.

Damballah (Haitian) Father god of wisdom (mandala) and reassurance (maze or labyrinth). Honor him with living plants.

Deive (Lithuanian) A stone deity particularly helpful when you wish to make rock patterns. All stones are sacred to him.

Diana (Roman) Goddess of the moon (labyrinth) and nature (hedge or garden patterns). Honor her with moonstones or jasmine incense.

Dolma, White Tara (Tibet) Goddess who blends human and divine characteristics (mandala). Honor her with lion imagery, lotus flower, or patterns with seven points.

Dua (Egyptian) The personification of today, and the reminder from the mandala to live presently and attentively.

Ea (Chaldean) God of wisdom (mandala) and magick (all). Honor him with salt water.

Echua (Yucatan) The god of travelers who can bless the path ahead.

Evander (Roman) The bearer of the Greek alphabet, call on him to help with word patterns and honor him with books.

Fa (Benin) God of destiny which is not fixed. This god helps us live beyond the border of the mandala.

Filia Vocis (Latin) Goddess of the voice, perfect for helping with mantras and incantations. Also an oracular being. Honor her with verbalization or song.

Flora (Roman) Goddess of all plant life (hedge and garden patterns). Honor her with vines and flowers.

Ganesa (Indian) God of removing obstacles whose energy can help with any patterned work that seems difficult in formulating. Honor him with elephant images.

Gou (Benin) Moon god who offers us a masculine balance to the feminine energy of the labyrinth. Honor him with chameleons or silver items.

Grian (Irish) A fair queen (maze). Honor her with solar imagery.

Halki (Hittite) A corn god who might be called upon in making maize mazes. Honor him with wine or barley.

Hanuman (Hindu) God of learning (maze). Honor him with sandalwood incense.

Harmonia (Greek) Goddess of harmony and love (mandala). Honor her with love charms or snake imagery.

Hathor (Egyptian) Goddess who embodies the ultimate feminine qualities (labyrinth). Honor her with music or dance.

Hatif (Arabic) The spirit of good advice and directions (all). Honor him with an oil lamp.

Hecate (Greek) Goddess of crossroads (maze) and patroness to witches (all). Honor her with hazel wood, almonds, or myrrh.

Hotei (Japanese) God of laughter and joy (all). Honor him with linen.

Hsi-Ho (Chinese) Goddess of suns (blending maze/labyrinth energy). Honor her with ten-pointed/segmented patterns.

Hun Ten (Chinese) God of chaos before order (maze).

Ida (Hindu) Goddess who teaches various occult secrets including divination, word power (written patterns), and breath (mandala). Honor her with lunar items.

Iris (Greek) Goddess of the rainbow who bears messages from earth to heaven (mandala or exit path of labyrinth). Honor her with honied breads.

Isara (Mesopotamian) Goddess of oaths (labyrinth or maze) and of good judgement (maze). Honor her with snake imagery.

Istar (Babylonian) Goddess of love whose name means "star." Call on her when making eight-pointed mandalas (which are particularly suited to relationship work or self-love).

Itzamna (Mayan) God who taught writing (any word mandala) and the use of maize (mazes). Honor him with images of a squirrel.

Janus (Roman) God of doorways and gatekeeper of heaven, call on Janus to watch over your comings and goings. Honor him with musk incense or two-sided items, like coins.

Kaukas (Lithuanian) Guardian spirit of treasure and luck, call on the Kaukas when you wish to unlock a great gift. Honor this spirit with dragon images.

K'uei (Chinese) God of tests (maze). Honor him with any study items.

Kunado (Japanese) God of the road, specifically the pathways not to take (maze). Honor him with maps.

Kwan Yin (Chinese) Goddess of healing, magick, and fertility (mandala). Honor her with lotus flowers or lion images.

Laverna (Italian) Goddess of trickery (maze). Honor her with a libation poured from your left hand.

Lug (Celtic) God of magickal arts and all handcrafts, Lug can help you express metaphysical creativity in your patterns. Honor him with fresh bread.

Ma'at (Egyptian) Goddess of justice, truth, law, and order (maze and mandala). Honor her with a red feather.

Macuilxochitl (Mexican) God of games who can help with maze work. Honor him with spring flowers.

Mama Pacha (Incan) Earth goddess who gave birth to universal creativity (mandala). Honor her with living plants.

Meni (Chaldean) Goddess of love and fate (labyrinth). Honor her with an offering of your favorite beverage.

Metis (Greek) Goddess of wisdom (mandala) and good counsel (maze). Honor her with pregnant goddess images.

Minos (Greek) The god of the Cretan bull cult, who is considered a totemic masculine symbol. While his story is associated with the labyrinth, Minos became the judge of the underworld after death and is connected with the Justice card of the Tarot, making him a good god for maze work. Honor him with aloe.

Mithra (Persian) God of light, purity, and victory (mandala). Honor him by working in a sunny region or wearing yellow/gold items.

Moerae (Greek) Goddesses of fate and destiny (mandala or labyrinth). Honor them with thread or yarn.

Morpheus (Greek) God of dreams suited to helping you with patterned dream work.

Nabu (Assyro-Babylonian) God of scribes (written patterns) and wisdom (mandala).

Nahmauit (Egyptian) Goddess who removes evil or negativity (the path into the labyrinth). Honor her with images of a sistrum.

Nataraja (Hindu) God of dance (labyrinth). Honor him with rhythmic percussion.

Neith (Egyptian) Personification of the active female powers of the universe (labyrinth). Honor her with woven items.

Nerthus (Teutonic) Earth and peace goddess (mandala). Honor her with a sheathed sword or dagger tied into the hilt.

Ninkarrak (Chaldean) Goddess of healing (mandala), and who eliminates bad luck (path out of the labyrinth).

Norns (Teutonic) see **Moerae.**

Odin (Scandinavian) God of cunning (maze), magick, and poetry (mandala). Honor him with rainwater.

Olwyn (Welsh) Goddess who represents the trial of the Virgin Dance (maze/labyrinth). Honor her with May flowers.

Pan (Greek) God of nature and woodlands who can help with any grown pattern efforts. Honor him with orchids and patchouli.

Pingala (Hindu) Goddess who embodies a cosmic force for manifestation (the exit of the labyrinth or living beyond the mandala). Honor her with twelve-point motifs, especially zodiacal ones.

Pukkeenegak (Eskimo) Goddess of providence (all). Honor her with painted body patterns.

Pushan (Hindu) God who rules over life's network (mandala and labyrinth). Honor him with solar imagery.

Quetzalcoatl (Aztec) God of practical knowledge who will help you apply the mandala's lesson or get through the maze. Honor him with feathers.

Ra Nambasanga (Fijian) A bisexual deity (mandala). Honor this being with balanced or two-sided items.

Ratis (British) Goddess of the fortress (exterior wall of all patterns). Honor her with sturdy building items (like wood or brick).

Sanjna (Hindu) Goddess of agreement (mandala) and consciousness (maze). Honor her with three-pointed motifs or horse imagery.

Sarasvati (Hindu) Goddess of speech (mandala), knowledge (maze), and the arts (all). Honor her with fresh flowers or drumming.

Saturn (Roman) God of planting who can help with grown patterns. Honor him with ash, yew, myrrh, and seeds.

Saules Meitas (Latvian) Daughters of the sun who sew roses (the labyrinth's center and the point of the mandala). Honor them with dew water.

Savitar (Hindu) God of movement (mandala and labyrinth). Honor him with golden-colored clothing.

Shakti (Nepalese/Tibetan) The ultimate feminine principle in motion (labyrinth). Honor her with sacred dances.

Shekinah (Hebrew) Goddess of wisdom and illumination (mandala). Honor her with any source of light or fire.

Shing-mu (Chinese) Goddess of perfected intelligence (maze). Honor her with books or other symbols of learning.

Silvanus (Roman) God guardian of boundaries [the exterior line of the pattern]. Honor him with wildflowers.

Sin (Chaldean) God of time (mandala and labyrinth). Honor him with silver items or lapis (not to be confused with the Teutonic goddess by the same name who presides over truth).

Sodasi (Hindu) Goddess of perfection and beauty (mandala). Honor her with lotus flowers or blue items.

Sorya (Slavonic) Warrior goddess who can help you fight the good fight (all). Honor her with water.

Spes (Roman) Goddess of gardens and personification of hope. Call on her when making hedge mazes and labyrinths, or when designing a flower mandala. Honor her with flowers and grains.

Sphynx (Egyptian and Greek) Guardians of treasures, the sphynx are masters of riddles, making them wholly suited to maze work.

Taliesen (Welsh) A great bard known for his riddles. Call on this spirit with music or song when you need insights into maze work.

Tashmit (Chaldean) Goddess of letters (written patterns), prayer (all), and learning (maze). Honor her with written words.

Terminus (Roman) Fixer of boundaries. If the edge of your mandala is "off" this is a good personification to call upon. Honor him with simple stones.

Themis (Greek) Goddess of balance (mandala) and good advice (maze). Honor her with an offering of any elixir.

Tien (Chinese) Once this god guarded the vault of heaven, then he became the vault (mandala).

Toma (Tibetan) Goddess of intellect (maze), honor her with dance or red-colored items.

Tyr (Teutonic) Law-giving god (labyrinth) who also is the patron of athletes (maze). Honor him with the rune of the same name (looks like an arrow pointing upward).

Ullr (Icelandic) God of archery who will help you hit your mark (mandala and labyrinth). Honor him with snow or sky-blue items.

Urutaetae (Tahitian) God of games (maze) and dance (labyrinth). Dancing is a suitable way to invoke this god.

Vach (Hindu) Goddess of speech, specifically mantras (mandala). Honor her with milk.

Vanth (Etruscan) Spirits who help with matters of death, suited to summerland labyrinth rituals.

Wepwwer (Egyptian) Opener of the way (all). Honor him with yellow items.

Xochiquetzal (Aztec) Goddess who presides over flowers and dance (labyrinth). Honor her with woven items.

Yachimato-Hime (Japanese) Goddess of many roads (maze).

Yamni (Lakota) God of games (maze) and dance (labyrinth). Honor him by opening a window to let in fresh winds.

Mazes, Mandalas, and Labyrinths of the World

*Thou mayst not wander in that labyrinth, there minotaurs
and ugly reasons lurk*

—Shakespeare, *King Henry VI*

Despite the great Bard's warnings, you may indeed want to wander in the halls, or gaze upon, some of the world's labyrinths, mazes, and mandalas. For those of you with gypsy souls aching to travel, here is but a brief sampling of the sacred patterns you can see "on the road."

Sites

Albright Art Gallery, Buffalo, NY Houses a videotape of the creation of a mandala from start to finish, as done by visiting Tibetan monks.

Amiens Cathedral, France A labyrinth built in gothic style around 1288 and restored in the 1800s.

Angels Nest Labyrinth, Oxford, NC 919-693-3229. This is a privately owned labyrinth made from brick and mulch. Open weekends from 12–6, and other times by appointment.

Arkville Maze, New York State A brick maze with bronze images of a minotaur, Daedalus, and Icarus.

Ashcombe Maze, Victoria, Australia Located at Shoreham, this is an archetypal hedge maze.

Bayeux Cathedral, France A twelfth–thirteenth-century gothic-styled labyrinth.

Bishop Quarterman Conference Center, Amarillo, TX 806-383-6878. Made from brick and glass, you can get more information by e-mailing ricck@aol.com.

Blenheim Palace, Southern England This is the world's largest symbolic hedge maze, depicting various military victories in yew.

Bloise, France Roman thermal baths of Verdes featuring a labyrinth on the east wing.

Borobudur, Java Constructed around A.D. 800, this Buddhist monument was an important spiritual center that is still being restored. Taking the form of a mandala-styled step pyramid, this site has three stupas (circular levels) and six rectangular passageways (connecting it also to labyrinth patterns), which together are said to represent the layout of the universe.

On your way up, you will have to ascend ten levels, each of which represents a different stage of spiritual growth. You will also circle the temple nine times before you reach the top—the point of the mandala, and the place of perfection.

Braemore Mizmaze, Hampshire, England A turf maze located in the middle of a quiet woods.

Callanish, Scotland A standing stone mandala where ancient rites of marriage were performed among other Druidic traditions.

Casa Grande, AZ Early Native American drawings here feature labyrinths that tell mythic stories of the people who lived here.

Cathedral at Chartres France A 42-foot circumference, eleven-circuit design, 294 meters in total length, with lunation laid in marble on the floor of this magnificent medieval church. Particularly powerful for engaging one's intuitive self. May have been a type of lunar calendar in early history.

Cathedral of San Martino, Lucca Built in the 1200s, the

western portico on the north side of the bell tower houses a 50-cm labyrinth chiseled in stone.

Cawdor Castle, Inverness, Scotland The site of King Duncan's murder is also the home of a holly hedge maze done in Roman mosaic pattern.

Chapel Manor, England Built in 1830, this holly hedge maze includes fountains, statues, and a centralized courtyard.

Chateau de Thoiry, France An intricate maze whose overview reveals an eye, images of the five senses, an elephant, obelisks, an owl, fish, dove, lizard, and nine bridges! This particular maze is dedicated to the energies of art, science, and love.

Chatworth Hedge Maze, England Built in the nineteenth century, this hedge maze was recently open for public tours.

Cheju Island, South Korea This hedge maze was commissioned by the local university. It includes a huge human statue and a waterfall.

Chenies Manor House, England A hedge maze haunted by the spirit of Henry VII looking for his adulterous wife, Catherine Howard with her lover Thomas Culpepper, who purportedly met there for trysts.

Coconut Creek, Panama City, FL A two-mile fence maze that covers a full mile of land.

Comerod, Switzerland This town houses a Roman mosaic labyrinth.

Copiegne, France A limestone relief featuring a labyrinth with Daedalus and Icarus dating to approximately the seventeenth century.

Dome of the Rock, Jerusalem This golden dome sacred to Muslim followers was set up using very detailed mathematical calculations. The dome has sixteen points equidistant from the center, which is the mythical center of the world (in other words, a perfect mandala). This site accentuates energy for prayer or any personal pilgrimage you wish to undertake.

Dragon Labyrinth, Cornwall, England Located in the Newquay Zoo.

Earth Wisdom Labyrinth A 93-foot labyrinth located in Elgin, Illinois, at the Unitarian Universalist Church (847-888-0668). This particular piece is dedicated to experiencing natural/earth energies.

Ely Cathedral A pavement maze in southern England built in the 1870s. This is actually a deceptive labyrinth, having only one path.

Glastonbury Tor A fourteenth-century church that lies atop a gently sculpted mandala landscape. Walking the grounds here generates energy for prayerfulness, faith, and healing.

Glendurgan Hedge Maze, England This hedge maze is planted in laurel, and was designed in 1833.

Grace Cathedral Center for Wholeness, San Francisco, CA Patterned after the Chartres Cathedral design in France.

Hampton Court Hedge Maze West of London, this maze was laid out in the 1600s. There is also a copy of this maze at Tatton Park Knutsford, Cheshire.

Hemkund Valley of Flowers, India Nature's mandala in full bloom, this valley has over two hundred types of flowers and the region is considered sacred to the Sikhs.

Hilton Maze, Cambridgeshire, England The stone pillar in the center of this turf maze was cut in 1660, but the site may be much older.

Julian's Bower, Alkborough, England A thirteenth-century turf maze.

Kangru, Himachel Pradsh A mandala made in the eighteenth century that was used to calculate astronomical periods and as a meditation aid.

Labyrinth Center, Fairveiw, NC A seven-circuit, Cretan-styled labyrinth (e-mail: labyrinthkeepers@worldnet.att.net).

Lapa Maze, Cornwall, England Made in 1804, this maze creates an image from overhead of the first locomotive. With this in mind, it might be a suitable maze to walk to get your life moving and conscious self motivated!

Leeds Castle, England A hedge maze that bears various Christian overtones and has a lovely seashell-studded exit tunnel.

Longleat House Located in southern England, this estate has visually stunning mazes made from hedge, stone, bush, and grass depicting the sun and moon. One maze is the world's longest, having six bridges, and spiral junctures.

Louisiana Children's Museum Contains a color maze.

Lucca Cathedral, Italy A twelfth–thirteenth-century gothic-styled labyrinth.

Mirepoix Cathedral, France A twelfth–thirteenth-century gothic-styled labyrinth.

Mount Meru, China Galleries and museums in this area often house three-dimensional mandalas in precious metal. These incredible pieces of art were used for meditation, communion, and as offerings to the Mountain.

Nazca Lines, Peru Some of these patterns have maze- or labyrinth-like imagery dating to the fifth–thirteenth century A.D.

Nepal The museums in this area often house books and manuscripts of ancient mandalas.

New Harmony Hedge Maze, ID Designed to depict the difficulty in achieving unity, and the beauty that harmony creates, this was made in 1939.

Norton Museum of Art, FL In this museum 13,500 clay bricks in six different colors create a maze depicting Theseus and the Minotaur in the center.

Omphalos, Greece Part of the sacred Delphic site, this is the "point" of a great prophetic mandala and the center of an earth-generated labyrinth that represents our eternal heritage. As a side note, many people believe that the cliffs of Greece may hold as-yet undiscovered labyrinths that were once a delphic stronghold and political refuge.

Painted Desert, AZ The petroglyphs in this region show a mandala-styled spiral pilgrimage of both the Hopi people and the Kachina spirits who guide and protect them.

Peaugres Safari Park, France Includes a Dragon Mirror Maze complete with holograms, mirrors, and aquariums.

Rad Labyrinth Located in Hannover, Germany, this is a nine-circuit labyrinth.

Ravenna, San Vitale A black and white marble seven-circuit labyrinth made in the sixteenth century and domed.

Reparatus Basilica, Orleansville, France A Romanesque labyrinth built in 324 A.D. showing the church at the center as a guiding force in the spiritual life of a person.

Russborough House, Ireland A lovely hedge maze with a pillar in the center topped by cupid. A marvelous site for love rites.

Saffron Walden Located in Essex, England, this turf maze has a strong medieval appeal, complete with a one-mile path fashioned from sculpted earthworks. Very possibly a marriage maze in the eighteenth century.

Salzburg, Austria This town houses a 21-foot by 18-foot Roman mosaic maze.

San Pietro di Conflentu, La Spexia, Italy A relief labyrinth on sandstone slab is all that remains of this ancient cloister. This is a Christianized version in which Christ replaces the minotaur at the center of the labyrinth to symbolize Christ as the center of a believer's world, or perhaps reflecting his underworld journey and victory.

San Vitale, Ravena, Italy A sixth-century Byzantine labyrinth set in front of an altar.

Santa Marla Cathedral, Italy A twelfth–thirteenth-century cathedral in gothic style.

Seville, Spain This town houses a Roman mosaic patterned labyrinthian style maze with ropelike boards to represent Ariadne's Thread.

Sjoborg Circle, Sola, Norway An ancient stone mandala circle that was used as a meeting place. It depicted the eight-spoked wheel and bore twenty-four standing stones.

St. Agnes, Scilly Islands Houses a rock labyrinth laid in 1729 and later restored called "Troy Town."

St. Lucca Cathedral, Italy A ninth-century labyrinth on the wall is still traced to this day before entering the sanctuary as a tool for improved meditative focus and spiritual awareness.

St. Quentin, France Pavement maze in the shape of a maltese cross, possibly created by Knights of St. John after crusades.

Stonehenge, England A standing stone mandala of druidic and astrological significance.

Sweed's Ring Located in Steigra, Germany this is a turf labyrinth with eleven circuits.

Three Land's Point Maze, Netherlands Features fountains, bridges, and images suited to the three countries on which it borders (the other two being Germany and Holland).

Trastavere Cathedral, Rome A twelfth–thirteenth-century cathedral in gothic style.

Tudor Rose Maze Located in Kentwell Hall, Suffolk, England this is the largest brick maze in the world.

Val Camonica Located in Northern Italy, this is a rock-carved labyrinth.

Varmlands Saby (Sweden) A maze that includes a portrait of Eve on one side, Adam on the other, and the Tree of Life between them with a sun overhead. It was made in 1979 and suitably entitled *Creation.*

Villa Pisani Tower Maze, Stra, Italy A garden created in 1720 containing an image of Minerva who stands atop the central view tower.

Vironica's Maze A lovely brick and grass maze with soft curving turns. Located in Parham Park, southern England.

West Boutan A fresco in the Temple Court of Paro Dzong fortress houses a beautiful cosmic mandala repressing the movement of the universe.

Williamsburgh Maze, VA Neatly nestled into the grounds of the Governor's House, this maze was built in 1935.

Winding Path, Stolp, Poland This has nineteen rings and was for many years the site of a tri-annual shoemakers festival. I cannot help but wonder if their dancing was meant to invoke the fairy folk's aid in their arts!

Web Sources

manbymaril@aol.com: beautiful original mandalas produced on t-shirts, notecards, posters, bookmarks, candles, and other gift items. Special orders considered.

www.synergycenter.com: mandala work for personal growth

www.tibet.com: mandala exhibits along with Tibetan art

www.geocities.com/tokyo/towers/6714/page3.html: three-dimensional sand and painted mandalas

www.chron.com/mandala: time lapse photography of a Tibetan sand mandala as created by monks visiting Houston, Texas

www.songnet.com/mymandala: one pattern mandala cards and posters, the proceeds from which support breast cancer research

www.mandalas.com: heart center studio with amazing mandala paintings, posters, workshops, and lectures

BIBLIOGRAPHY

Aldington, Richard, trans. *New Larousse Encyclopedia of Mythology.* Middlesex, England: Hamlyn Publishing, 1973.

Arguelles, Jose and Miriam. *Mandala.* Boston: Shambhala Publications,1972.

Artress, Dr. Lauren. *Walking a Sacred Path.* New York: Riverhead Books, 1995.

Ann, Martha, and Dorothy Myers Imel. *Goddesses in World Mythology.* New York: Oxford University Press, 1995.

Arrien, Angeles. *The Four Fold Way.* New York: Harper Collins, 1993.

Beyerl, Paul. *Herbal Magick.* Custer, Wash.: Phoenix Publishing, 1998.

Bruce-Mitford, Miranda. *Illustrated Book of Signs and Symbols.* New York: D. K. Publishing, 1996.

Budge, E. A. Wallis. *Amulets and Superstitions.* Oxford, England: Oxford University Press, 1930.

Cavendish, Richard. *A History of Magic.* New York: Taplinger Publishing, 1979.

Cooper, J. C. *Symbolic and Mythological Animals.* London, England: Aqarian Press, 1992.

Cunningham, Scott. *Crystal, Gem and Metal Magic.* St. Paul, Minn.: Llewellyn Publications, 1995.

_____. *Encyclopedia of Magical Herbs.* St. Paul, Minn.: Llewellyn Publications, 1988.

_____. *Magic in Food.* St. Paul, Minn.: Llewellyn Publications, 1991.

Davison, Michael Worth, ed. *Everyday Life Through the Ages.* Pleasantville, N.Y.: Reader's Digest Association Ltd., 1992.

Fincher, Susanne. *Creating Mandalas.* Boston: Shambhala, 1991.

Fisher, A., and H. Lexton. *Secrets of the Maze.* London, England: Quarto Inc., 1997.

Gordon, Leslie. *Green Magic.* New York: Viking Press, 1977.

Gordon, Stuart. *Encyclopedia of Myths and Legends.* London, England: Headline Book Publishing, 1993.

Hall, Manly P. *Secret Teachings of All Ages.* Los Angeles: Philosophical Research Society, 1977.

Jaskolski, Helmut. *The Labyrinth.* Boston: Shambhala, 1997.

Jordan, Michael. *Encyclopedia of Gods.* New York: Facts on File, 1993.

Jung, Carl G. *Mandala Symbolism.* Princeton: Princeton University Press, 1959.

Kunz, George Frederick. *Curious Lore of Precious Stones.* New York: Dover Publications, 1971.

Leach, Maria, ed.: *Standard Dictionary of Folklore, Mythology, and Legend.* New York: Harper & Row, 1984.

Leach, Marjorie. *Guide to the Gods.* Santa Barbara, Cal.: ABC-Clio, 1992.

Lurker, Manfred. *Dictionary of Gods and Goddesses, Devils and Demons.* New York: Routledge & Kegan Paul, 1995.

Matthews, W. H. *Mazes and Labyrinths: Their History and Development.* New York: Dover Publications, 1970.

Miller, Gustavus Hindman: *Ten Thousand Dreams Interpreted.* Chicago: M. A. Donhouse & Co., 1931.

Rudiger, Dahlke. *Mandalas of the World.* New York: Sterling Publishing, 1992.

Sjoo, Monica, and Barbara Mor. *The Great Cosmic Mother.* San Francisco: Harper & Row, 1987.

Telesco, Patricia: *Folkways.* St. Paul, Minn.: Llewellyn Publications, 1995.

––––––. *Futuretelling.* Freedom, Cal.: Crossing Press, 1997.

––––––. *Herbal Arts.* Secaucus, N.J.: Citadel Books, 1997.

––––––. *Kitchen Witch's Cookbook.* St. Paul, Minn.: Llewellyn Publications, 1994.

––––––. *The Language of Dreams.* Freedom, Cal.: Crossing Press, 1997.

––––––. *Witch's Brew.* St. Paul, Minn.: Llewellyn Publications, 1995.

Walker, Barbara. *The Woman's Dictionary of Symbols and Sacred Objects.* San Francisco: Harper & Row, 1988.

Waring, Philippa. *The Dictionary of Omens and Superstitions.* Secaucus, N.J.: Chartwell Books, 1978.

Wasserman, James. *Art and Symbols of the Occult.* Rochester, Vt.: Destiny Books, 1993.

Westwood, Jennifer. *Sacred Journies.* New York: Henry Holt and Company, 1997.